# Suit Contracts

T0154900

# D & B Publishing

New and forthcoming books.

## D & B Poker

| | | |
|---|---|---|
| 1-904468-06-3 | *Poker on the Internet* | Andrew Kinsman |
| 1-904468-08-X | *How Good is your Pot-Limit Hold'em?* | Stewart Reuben |
| 1-904468-07-1 | *How Good is your Pot-Limit Omaha?* | Stewart Reuben |

## D & B Bridge

| | | |
|---|---|---|
| 1-904468-09-8 | *Defensive Plays* | Sally Brock |
| 1-904468-00-4 | *No Trump Contracts* | David Bird |

## D & B Puzzles

| | | |
|---|---|---|
| 1-904468-03-9 | *200 Word Puzzles* | Carter and Russell |
| 1-904468-02-0 | *400 IQ Puzzles* | Carter and Russell |
| 1-904468-10-1 | *Solving IQ Puzzles* | Carter and Russell |
| 1-904468-11-X | *Solving Word Puzzles* | Carter and Russell |
| 1-904468-05-5 | The Times *Two Brains* | Keene and Jacobs |

## D & B General

| | | |
|---|---|---|
| 1-904468-13-6 | *Online Gambling* | Angus Dunnington |

D & B Publishing, PO Box 18, Hassocks, West Sussex BN6 9WR, UK
Tel: 01273 834680, Fax: 01273 831629, e-mail: info@dandbpublishing.com,
Website: www.dandbpublishing.com

# suit contracts

**Brian Senior**

D&B PUBLISHING

www.dandbpublishing.com

First published in 2003 by D & B Publishing, PO Box 18, Hassocks,
West Sussex BN6 9WR

Copyright © 2003 Brian Senior

The right of Brian Senior to be identified as the author of this work has been
asserted in accordance with the Copyrights, Designs and Patents Act 1988.

All rights reserved. No part of this publication may be reproduced, stored in a
retrieval system or transmitted in any form or by any means, electronic,
electrostatic, magnetic tape, photocopying, recording or otherwise, without prior
permission of the publisher.

**British Library Cataloguing-in-Publication Data**
A catalogue record for this book is available from the British Library.

ISBN 1-904468-01-2

All sales enquiries should be directed to:
D & B Publishing, PO Box 18, Hassocks, West Sussex BN6 9WR, UK
Tel: 01273 834680, Fax: 01273 831629, e-mail: info@dandbpublishing.com,
Website: www.dandbpublishing.com

Cover design by Horatio Monteverde.
Production by Navigator Guides.
Printed and bound in Great Britain by Biddles Ltd.

# Contents

# Introduction

To a far greater extent than any other aspect of the game of bridge, declarer play is something that can be practiced and improved with the aid of books. Of course, the books have to be used properly. It is of little value to read a book on declarer play as though it were a novel, just for entertainment. No, if you want to get the maximum benefit then it is necessary to put some work into your reading. Work through each example until you can see why the recommended play is correct. Where a problem is presented, do your best to work out the correct answer before turning to the solution. Though you are unlikely to ever pick up exactly the same hand in real life as those you have worked on in the book, still, the experience gained from the book makes it more likely that you will not only be able to recognise a particular situation at the table, but also that you will be familiar with and capable of executing the correct technique to solve your real-life play problem.

In this book I look at some of the techniques involved in successful play of suit contracts. Of course, some of these techniques will also apply in a no-trump contract, but there are many that are unique to suit contracts.

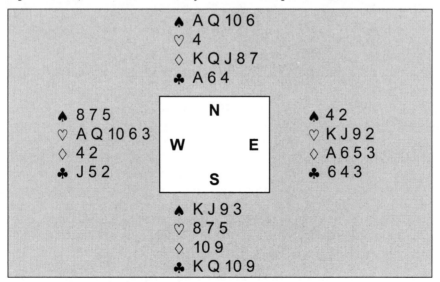

Why do we seek to find a trump fit with partner rather than just play every hand in no-trump? The first advantage of having a trump suit is that it offers a certain measure of control. Take this example:

North/South have 25 High Card Points between them, enough to play a game contract. Alas, if they play in Three No-trumps they will lose five heart tricks plus the ace of diamonds – two down, despite having twelve eventual winners available. Four Spades, however, is a simple matter, with declarer just losing to the two red aces and coming home with an overtrick. The difference is that North's trumps take care of the second and, if necessary, subsequent rounds of hearts.

The second benefit of playing a trump contract is that sometimes many more tricks can be created by ruffing. This second example illustrates just such a possibility:

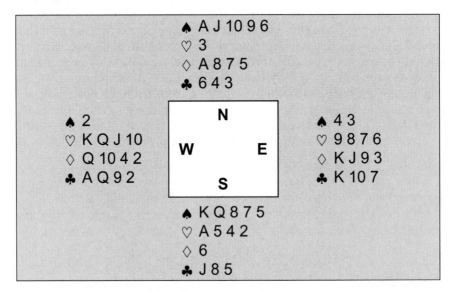

This time North/South have only 19 HCP between them, well short of the traditionally accepted requirements for bidding and making a game contract. And indeed, were they to attempt to play in Three No-Trumps, they would be held to just seven tricks, five spades plus the two red aces. But Four Spades is again a very different affair. The defenders can take three club winners but that is all. As soon as declarer gains the lead he commences to cash the red aces and simply ruff alternately hearts in the North hand and diamonds in the South hand until he has exhausted himself of both these suits. He comes to ten tricks with no difficulty at all thanks to the benefits of having a good trump suit and the power of distribution.

This book is broken up into ten chapters, each dealing with a different aspect of declarer play in suit contracts. The early chapters deal with relatively basic techniques, though they are no less important for that, while the later chapters handle some more advanced concepts. While the later techniques may appear to be more exciting, they are, if you like, the icing on the cake. A player who was expert in the earlier topics could be a good competent declarer without knowing about some of the more exotic techniques discussed later on. However, to be expert in the later techniques would be of little value to a player who did not have a firm grasp on the earlier, more basic ideas – rather like a building without firm foundations.

While this book is divided into ten sections, it is almost impossible to divorce one aspect of declarer play technique from all the others. In some instances a deal may appear as though it would be equally at home in a different section. Counting and planning are, for example, two concepts that are relevant to every hand. Try to play a successful squeeze without counting the hand out, or a trump coup without planning the play, and you will see that it is almost impossible to do so.

The trick, of course, is not merely to learn and understand the various techniques discussed in these pages, it is also to develop the judgement and experience to know when to use and when not to use any given approach to the play.

Ideally, declarer should stop and make a plan before playing the first card from dummy at trick one. Sometimes that plan may have to be fairly flexible, according to how things go in the early stages of the play and defence, and perhaps it will be necessary to switch to Plan B, or even Plan C, later on. Nonetheless, it is fair to say that even a poor plan is likely to be better than playing one trick at a time without any plan at all. Though it is something of a cliché, it is also true to say that more contracts fail at trick one through thoughtless play than fail at trick thirteen, when the die was often cast many tricks earlier.

So, I hope that you enjoy reading this book, but don't enjoy it too much. Put in the work to solve the many problems, and this effort will hold you in good stead when you have to solve a similar problem at the table. Good luck.

# Chapter One

# Counting

- ♡ **Different Forms of Counting**
- ♡ **Immediate Losers**
- ♡ **Points to Remember**
- ♡ **Try it Yourself**

 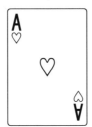 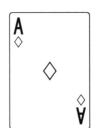 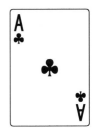

# Different Forms of Counting

Counting can take many forms. Declarer may count his winners or his losers, he may count the defenders' distribution as they follow or show out of each suit, and he may count the High Card Points with which each defender shows up.

The first thing to do when dummy appears, after thanking partner, of course, is to count your winners. This should be done in two stages; firstly count those immediately available, secondly those which can easily be made available, perhaps by simply knocking out a missing high card. Having got this far, we can then calculate how many extra winners we need to find and can look to see from where they might come. Counting the winners may not always be quite as straightforward as one might imagine. Take this example:

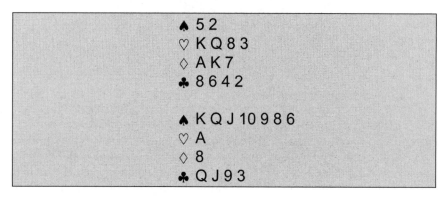

The contract is Four Spades and the opening lead is the queen of diamonds. As always, you start by counting your tricks. There are only five immediate winners, three hearts and two diamonds, but six more can be established simply by knocking out the ace of trumps, apparently making eleven in all. So there is no problem in making Four Spades, is there? Well, actually, there is. The problem is that there is a blockage in the heart suit and, now that your diamond entry to the North hand has been knocked out by the opening lead, you can count only one heart winner – the ace. That brings your total number of winners down to only nine, unless...

There is a solution, and it simply requires that you stop to think for a moment to make a plan. The key to finding the winning play is to appreciate that you do not actually need eleven tricks to make Four Spades; you need ten. That means you can afford to throw away one winner and still succeed in bringing home your contract. At trick one you win the ace of diamonds then, at trick two, cash the king of diamonds and throw away the blocking ace of hearts! Instead of having three heart winners, as at first glance, or only one heart winner as at second glance, you can now cash two hearts, North's king and queen. On these two winners you will pitch two clubs from the South hand and can then switch your attention to the trump suit. Ten tricks and the contract duly made.

## Immediate Losers

Sometimes, counting winners is not enough. Take a look at this next example:

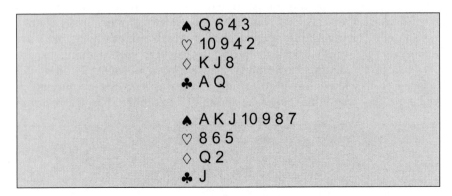

You play in Four Spades on the lead of the two of trumps, East following with the other missing trump. There are eight immediate tricks, seven spades plus the ace of clubs, and two more can easily be established in diamonds. That brings the total to ten; just what is required to make Four Spades. But if declarer wins the first trick and plays on diamonds, he is in serious danger of going down. Why? Count the number of immediate losers. When a defender takes the ace of diamonds he can switch to hearts and, unless there is an unlikely blockage, the defence can take three tricks in that suit, bringing their total to four. The contract is one down, with the established diamond tricks coming too late to be of any value.

Declarer's best chance to make his contract is not to play on diamonds but to take the club finesse at trick two. True, if the king is offside a heart switch will lead to defeat by two tricks, but if it succeeds declarer can then cash the club ace and throw away a heart loser. Now he can afford to lose the lead by playing on diamonds, but not before that heart has been disposed of.

Counting winners and losers is an essential part of the planning of the play of virtually every contract. Counting out the distribution of the opponents' hands is another valuable technique that can help to improve the odds on a successful 'guess' later in the play.

It is always worth taking a little extra care in a slam contract. How should Seven Spades be played on this combination after the lead of the two of spades, East following with the four?

```
                    ♠ K J 9 3
                    ♡ A J 2
                    ◇ A Q J
                    ♣ K 10 8

                    ♠ A Q 10 7
                    ♡ K Q 10
                    ◇ K 10 4
                    ♣ A J 6
```

Declarer wins the opening lead and draws the remainder of the missing trumps. He may think that it is just a guess as to which defender will hold the missing queen and, at this moment, he may well be correct. It can hardly do any harm to attempt to improve the odds in favour of a successful decision by delaying the play of the club suit for as long as possible.

Say that West turned up with three trumps to East's two. Declarer cashes the three heart winners and three diamond winners, then pauses to take stock. If both defenders have followed to three rounds of each red suit, then little information has been gained. But suppose that, while both follow to three rounds of diamonds, East shows out on the third round of hearts, marking himself with only two cards in the suit to West's five. At this point West is known to have started with three spades, five hearts and at least three diamonds – the location of the final diamond is unknown. That leaves West with at most two cards in clubs; therefore East has at least five club cards.

While there are no guarantees, East is far more likely to hold the queen of clubs than is West. Far from being a 50-50 proposition, as it was at the beginning, it is now at least five-to-two, or over 70%, that East will hold the club queen, and declarer should cash dummy's club king then lead low and finesse the jack.

Counting the defenders' points can also resolve what would otherwise be tricky guesses for declarer and it is not only bids that are actually made that provide crucial evidence. Consider also the evidence provided by what does not happen. Try this one:

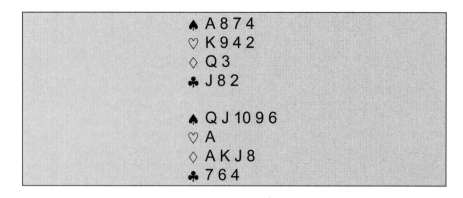

♠ A 8 7 4
♡ K 9 4 2
◊ Q 3
♣ J 8 2

♠ Q J 10 9 6
♡ A
◊ A K J 8
♣ 7 6 4

South declares Four Spades after opening in fourth seat after three passes. West kicks off with the ace, king and queen of clubs, followed by a switch to the heart jack. Missing four trumps to the king, the normal play would be to finesse. However, a moment's thought will show that the finesse cannot succeed. Why? Because West passed as dealer and has already turned up with 10 HCP – nine in clubs, one in hearts – so cannot hold the king of spades, as he would have opened the bidding if also holding that card. It may not look to be very good odds, but the only hope is to win the heart switch and lead a spade to the ace, praying for a singleton king with East.

You will find that there is something to count on pretty well every hand you ever play. Some of that counting of distribution and high cards can seem to be very hard work at first. There is no shortcut to being able to do all the necessary counting, but I can promise that it does get easier with time if you constantly try to do it.

## Points to Remember

- ♠ Always make a plan before playing to trick one. More contracts go down at trick one through playing too quickly than fail at trick thirteen.

- ♠ A key element of effective planning is to count one's winners and losers. Then one can look to see where the extra required tricks can be found.

- ♠ What seems to be a guess may often prove not to be so if declarer counts the opposing distribution and high cards, remembering what happened during the auction and, just as importantly, what did not.

# Try it Yourself

In each case you are declarer, sitting South. How should you play to give yourself the best possible chance to make your contract?

## Question 1

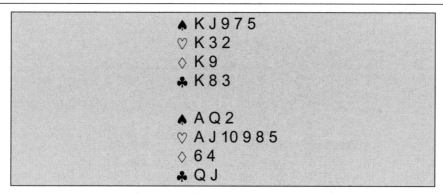

| West | North | East | South |
|------|-------|------|-------|
|      |       | 1◇   | 2♡    |
| Pass | 4♡    | All Pass |    |

West leads the jack of diamonds to the king and ace. East cashes the diamond queen then switches to ace and another club.

## Question 2

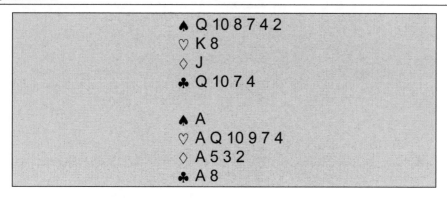

| West | North | East | South |
|------|-------|------|-------|
| 3◇   | Pass  | Pass | 4♡    |
| All Pass |    |      |       |

West leads the king of diamonds, East following.

## Question 3

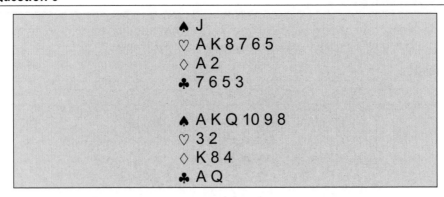

| West | North | East | South |
|------|-------|------|-------|
|  | 1♡ | Pass | 2♠ |
| Pass | 3♡ | Pass | 3♠ |
| Pass | 4♠ | Pass | 4NT |
| Pass | 5♡ | Pass | 5NT |
| Pass | 6◇ | Pass | 6♠ |
| All Pass |  |  |  |

West leads a small trump.

## Question 4

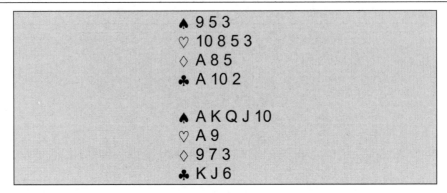

| West | North | East | South |
|------|-------|------|-------|
|  |  |  | 1♠ |
| 2♡ | 2♠ | Pass | 4♠ |
| All Pass |  |  |  |

West leads the king of hearts. Trumps are three-two, East having the length. Play on.

## Question 5

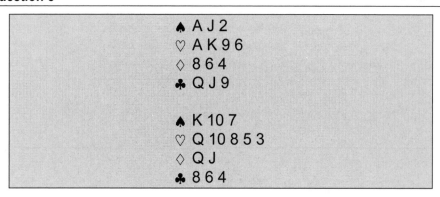

|       | ♠ A J 2      |       |       |
|-------|-------|-------|-------|
|       | ♡ A K 9 6    |       |       |
|       | ♢ 8 6 4      |       |       |
|       | ♣ Q J 9      |       |       |
|       |       |       |       |
|       | ♠ K 10 7     |       |       |
|       | ♡ Q 10 8 5 3 |       |       |
|       | ♢ Q J        |       |       |
|       | ♣ 8 6 4      |       |       |

| West  | North | East  | South |
|-------|-------|-------|-------|
|       |       | 1◊    | Pass  |
| Pass  | Dble  | 2♣    | 2♡    |
| 3◊    | 3♡    | All Pass |    |

West leads a low diamond and East wins the ace and returns the five to West's king. West plays a third diamond. Declarer ruffs low and draws trumps, finding that they are two-two, West having the jack. Play on.

## Question 6

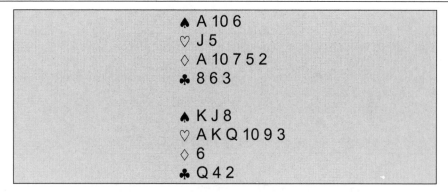

|       | ♠ A 10 6         |       |       |
|-------|-------|-------|-------|
|       | ♡ J 5            |       |       |
|       | ◊ A 10 7 5 2     |       |       |
|       | ♣ 8 6 3          |       |       |
|       |       |       |       |
|       | ♠ K J 8          |       |       |
|       | ♡ A K Q 10 9 3   |       |       |
|       | ◊ 6              |       |       |
|       | ♣ Q 4 2          |       |       |

| West  | North | East  | South |
|-------|-------|-------|-------|
|       |       |       | 1♡    |
| Pass  | 2◊    | Pass  | 3♡    |
| Pass  | 4♡    | All Pass |    |

West leads a low club to the ace and East returns a club to the queen and king. West cashes the club jack, East following, then switches to a low trump, East again following.

## Question 7

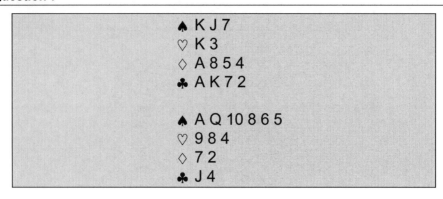

| West | North | East | South |
|------|-------|------|-------|
|      | 1♣    | Pass | 1♠    |
| Pass | 2NT   | Pass | 4♠    |
| All Pass | | | |

West leads the king of diamonds.

## Question 8

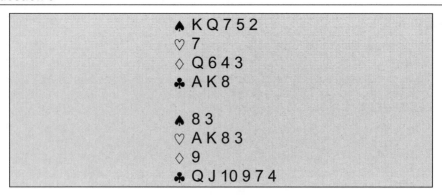

| West | North | East | South |
|------|-------|------|-------|
|      |       |      | 1♣    |
| Pass | 1♠    | Pass | 2♣    |
| Pass | 4♣    | Pass | 5♣    |
| All Pass | | | |

West leads the three of clubs.

## Question 9

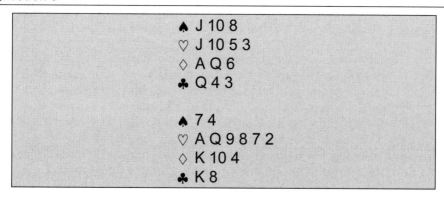

♠ J 10 8
♡ J 10 5 3
◇ A Q 6
♣ Q 4 3

♠ 7 4
♡ A Q 9 8 7 2
◇ K 10 4
♣ K 8

| West | North | East | South |
|------|-------|------|-------|
|      |       | 1NT(i) | 2♡ |
| Pass | 4♡ | All Pass | |

(i) 12-14

West leads the six of spades to the ten and queen. East continues with the ace and king of spades.

## Question 10

♠ A J 6
♡ J 6
◇ J 9 7
♣ Q 10 8 7 2

♠ Q 9 7 3
♡ A K Q 9 4
◇ Q 4
♣ A 5

| West | North | East | South |
|------|-------|------|-------|
|      |       |      | 1♡ |
| Pass | 2♣ | 2◇ | 2♠ |
| Pass | 3◇ | Pass | 3♡ |
| Pass | 4♡ | All Pass | |

West leads a diamond against Four Hearts and East wins and plays two more rounds of the suit. Declarer discards his club loser and is pleased to see West follow suit. When he draws trumps, East shows up with four. The spade finesse loses and back comes a diamond. Play on.

# Solutions

## Question 1

In Four Hearts, declarer wins the second round of clubs and should immediately attempt to draw the outstanding trumps. His only problem is to judge which defender is more likely to hold the trump queen. North/South have 27 HCP between them and West has already played the jack of diamonds, yet East opened the bidding. It is possible that East opened with only 10 HCP and a long diamond suit, but far more likely that he opened with 12 HCP, meaning that he has the heart queen. Best play is to play the heart king then lead low to the jack, playing East for queen to three or four cards.

## Question 2

Declarer has five possible losers: a club, a heart (if East has jack to four or five) and three diamonds; if he can ruff two diamonds that number will be reduced to three. So he wins the diamond ace and ruffs one – but if East can over-ruff with the jack and return a trump there will be no more ruffs and four eventual losers. The solution is simple once you see it. The first ruff should be with the king of trumps, back to the spade ace and ruff another diamond with the eight. If East over-ruffs, it is with the only possible defensive trump winner. Declarer makes six trumps in hand, one diamond ruff, and three aces.

## Question 3

Declarer has eleven top tricks and on any other lead could have played to ruff a diamond in dummy. Now that dummy's trump has been drawn, however, he must rely on either the club finesse or establishing the hearts. It is possible to combine the two chances. Draw trumps, then set about the hearts. But stop and count the winners! Only one extra trick is needed, so gambling on an even heart break is unnecessary. Playing ace, king and ruffing a heart may lead to defeat if the suit splits four-one and the club king is offside. Instead, duck a heart. Assuming that both defenders follow, the contract is secure. Win any return in hand and now play ace, king and ruff a heart. The ace of diamonds is the entry to cash the established winner. If hearts are five-zero, then the club finesse will be required.

## Question 4

No, this is not about counting the missing high cards to solve the riddle of where the queen of clubs is hiding, nor the defensive distribution. All declarer has to do is to count his tricks, of which he has nine on top. Win the ace of hearts, draw trumps and play back the nine of hearts. West wins, but now dummy's two aces permit declarer to play the heart ten, throwing a diamond loser from hand, and in the process establishing the heart eight as the game-going trick, then get back to dummy to cash it. A classic loser-on-loser play.

## Question 5

Declarer plays a club to the jack and king and East plays ace and another club, West producing the ten. Had East exited with a spade, picking up the queen of that suit, declarer would have had to play a second club himself. Knowing that East must have the club ace for his opening bid, the correct play would have been low to the nine. Now, however, the club position has been resolved but not the spade position. A distributional count suggests that West has five spades to East's two. Should declarer play West for the spade queen then? No. The bidding offers much more secure evidence. West passed his partner's opening bid and has already shown up with a king and a jack. Holding the spade queen also, he would have responded One Spade. It must be correct to play for the queen of spades with East.

## Question 6

If declarer simply runs the trumps, he will usually be left with a close to 50-50 spade guess. Perhaps he can improve those odds by discovering more about the defenders' distribution. Win the heart switch in hand and play ace and ruff a diamond, then cross to the jack of trumps and ruff another diamond, then run the trumps. Having seen three rounds of clubs, three rounds of diamonds and four rounds of trumps, declarer may know which defender is longer in spades. Whoever that defender is should be finessed against for the missing spade queen.

## Question 7

Most players would win the opening lead, cross to hand with a trump, and lead a heart to the king. Most players would be wrong, however. On a bad day, the heart ace is offside and East has three trumps. He returns one now, wins the second round of hearts and returns another trump, leaving none in the dummy to ruff the last heart.

The above line of play is the best one if eleven tricks are needed. In Four Spades only ten tricks are required and that is almost a sure thing. This would be an easy hand if dummy held two small hearts. Ignore the temptation of the king of hearts and simply play a heart off the dummy at trick two, just as you would if both hearts really were small cards, and, on regaining the lead, lead a second heart. Nothing can now prevent the third heart being ruffed in dummy.

## Question 8

Without the trump lead this would be an easy contract, as declarer would simply play to ruff both his losing hearts in the dummy. Unfortunately, if he wins the opening lead and plays three rounds of hearts, ruffing, he has no quick way back to hand to take the second ruff. As soon as he gives up the lead, the defence will play another trump, and that will be the end of dummy's ruffing power.

Trying for heart ruffs will provide only ten tricks so declarer looks for something better. The spade suit is the best bet. Win the trump lead in hand and lead to the spade king, not attempting to ruff hearts so as to retain dummy's trumps as later entries. If that loses and a trump comes back, play queen and another spade, ruffing. A three-three spade split will be required after drawing any outstanding trump. If the first spade scores, however, prospects are a little brighter. Cross to hand with a heart and play a second spade up. Whenever the ace is onside there will be two high spade winners. Ruffing a low spade will establish a third winner whenever the suit splits four-two or better, and three spade winners brings declarer's total to the eleven required.

## Question 9

While a finesse is the percentage play in the trump suit, missing as here three cards including the king, there is a significant possibility of a bare king offside. East has turned up with 9 HCP already and opened a weak No-trump, limiting himself to a maximum of 14 HCP in total. He must hold one of the club ace and heart king but not both if he is to be within his announced range. Having ruffed the third spade, declarer plays the king of clubs to smoke out the ace. If the king is allowed to hold, he plays a second round to the queen. If West shows up with the ace of clubs, declarer will take the normal play of the trump finesse with confidence. If, however, East has the ace of clubs, there is no room for him to hold the heart king also and declarer should lay down the trump ace. Actually, he can make this play with just as much confidence as when he takes the finesse in the other scenario. Why? Because East must have two hearts for his One No-trump opening, promising a balanced hand, which leaves West with only one, so the king is sure to drop.

## Question 10

Declarer ruffs the diamond return and his main hope appears to be to bring in the spades for three winners. It would be careless of him to simply play a spade to the ace and a spade back to his hand, however. It costs nothing to cash the ace of clubs first. As we will see in a later chapter, one possibility is that West started life with four spades to the ten plus the king of clubs. If so, he would have been squeezed on the previous trick and either had to unguard the spades or bare the king of clubs. In the latter case, cashing the club ace will provide a rich, if somewhat unexpected, bonus.

There is a second possibility, which is the one that occurred in real life. East showed out on the ace of clubs, marking him with precisely 4-4-5-0 distribution. If this is the case, it is a 100% play to cross to the ace of spades then lead low and finesse the spade nine at trick twelve. And if East follows to the ace of clubs? Then he cannot hold four spades as he has already shown up with at least ten cards in the other three suits. Now declarer plays a spade to the ace then back to the queen. Cashing the club allowed declarer to get an accurate count on the hand.

# Chapter Two

# All About Trumps

- ♡ **Drawing Trumps**
- ♡ **Communications**
- ♡ **Establishing the Side Suit**
- ♡ **Points to Remember**
- ♡ **Try it Yourself**

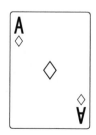

# Drawing Trumps

Having a trump suit has a number of advantages, including offering the possibility to make extra tricks by ruffing and of having greater control of the play. However, the defenders are also looking to take advantage of there being a trump suit – sometimes it is they who can take extra tricks by ruffing your winners. So we come to the most commonly asked question of all: Should I draw trumps?

Sometimes the answer is very easy to see. You may be in a position to make your contract by sheer weight of high cards and in that case should draw all the outstanding trumps is quickly as possible. This simple example would be a case in point:

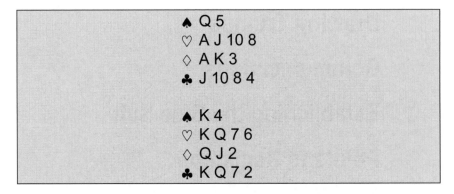

Playing Four Hearts on the lead of the eight of diamonds, it appears that the only way in which you can be defeated is if the defence manages to ruff out some of your high cards. Win the opening lead, draw as many rounds of trumps as are necessary, and the contract will make with an overtrick.

The reverse occurs when you have a great deal of work for your trump suit to do. Now you cannot afford to draw them at the start. Take this example:

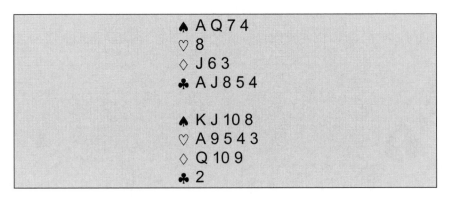

The king of hearts is led against your contract of Four Spades. Draw trumps and you will be left with well short of the required ten tricks. You need to do a lot of ruffing to create the extra tricks you need for your contract. Simply win the ace of hearts, cash the ace of clubs, and ruff clubs and hearts alternately until you run out of trumps. Unless the second round of one or other suit is over-ruffed by the spade nine, you will have ten tricks – just what is required.

The previous examples have illustrated the extremes, but sometimes the situation is not quite so clear. Look at this next example:

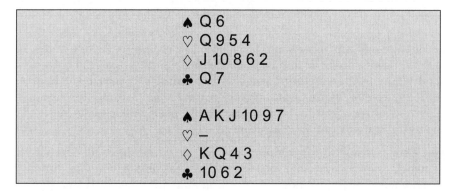

When West leads the ace of hearts against your contract of Four Spades it may appear that you have ten tricks simply by ruffing, drawing trumps and knocking out the ace of diamonds. True, you do have ten winners; unfortunately the defenders will cash three club tricks when they get in with the ace of diamonds and that will mean one down.

The solution is very simple, though you will require some good fortune. After ruffing the opening lead you must attempt to knock out the ace of diamonds before drawing trumps. The point is that now the defenders will be able to cash only two club winners because dummy's spades will take care of the third round. You need to do some work while the trump suit gives you control of an important side suit, hence cannot draw trumps until after that work has been done. And the good fortune that I mentioned? You will require that the missing diamonds divide evenly, two in each hand; otherwise the defence may take a diamond ruff to defeat you. Still, while that is a risk, it is one that you have to take, and is far less dangerous than trying to knock out the ace of diamonds *after* drawing trumps.

# Communications

Another reason not to draw trumps immediately may revolve around your communications. On this next deal it is essential that the side suit be established before drawing all the trumps.

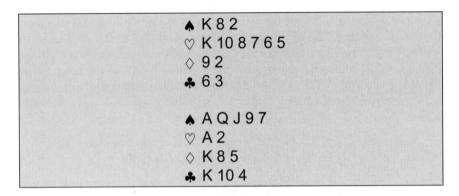

♠ K 8 2
♡ K 10 8 7 6 5
◇ 9 2
♣ 6 3

♠ A Q J 9 7
♡ A 2
◇ K 8 5
♣ K 10 4

The contract is Four Spades and the lead a low trump to the five and seven. By far and away the best chance to make this contract is to find both major suits dividing evenly, enabling you to first establish then cash the hearts. The alternative of trying to find minor-suit aces onside and later ruffing the third round of each suit in dummy looks quite poor, particularly as the defence has already begun to draw dummy's trumps.

If you draw all the missing trumps, you will no longer have an entry to the long hearts. Best is to cash a second trump, retaining the king in dummy. Now play ace of hearts, a heart to the king and ruff a heart. If that passes off peacefully, you can lead a spade to the king, drawing the last trump in the process, and cash the three established heart winners. Your later lead up to one of the minor-suit kings will merely be an attempt to make an overtrick. And if one or other major does not divide evenly, then it was very unlikely that any line of play would have succeeded.

## Establishing the Side Suit

Sometimes, the need to establish the side suit before drawing trumps is a matter of control rather than of communications. Take a look at this next hand:

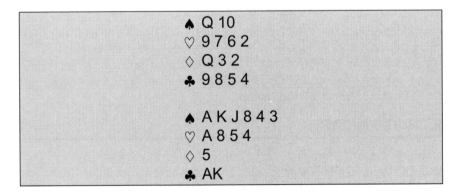

♠ Q 10
♡ 9 7 6 2
◇ Q 3 2
♣ 9 8 5 4

♠ A K J 8 4 3
♡ A 8 5 4
◇ 5
♣ A K

The contract is Four Spades and West leads ace and another diamond. You put up dummy's queen more in hope than expectation and, sure enough, East covers with the king, forcing you to ruff. Many players would draw trumps now then turn their attention to the heart suit, hoping to establish the tenth trick there on a three-two split. Those players would be playing the hand poorly. If the trumps split four-one declarer will go down because, after drawing trumps, he will have only one trump left and will have to give up the lead twice to establish the extra heart trick. Repeated diamond leads will leave the defence in control.

There is a solution. Where the above line requires even splits in both majors, the four-one spade break can be overcome. It is only the three-two heart break that is essential for success. Declarer should ruff at trick two, then play ace and another heart. Ruffing the next diamond play, he should play a third round of hearts. Assuming hearts to have split three-two, that establishes the tenth trick, and if they do not divide favourably then the contract cannot be made. However, if the defence now plays a fourth round of diamonds, it can be ruffed in dummy, the short trump hand, which still leaves declarer with four trumps to draw the missing ones. A little foresight brings home a contract that might fail on thoughtless play.

## Points to Remember

♠ Having a trump suit offers a number of advantages including offering the prospect of making extra tricks by ruffing, but never forget that the defenders can also take extra tricks by ruffing. When to draw trumps is often a crucial decision.

♠ Declarer must always attempt to retain trump control, sometimes allowing the defenders to win a possibly unnecessary trick to ensure this.

♠ Always take care to ensure that you have the necessary communications between the two hands to allow your plan of campaign to succeed.

♠ It often pays to establish the side-suit before setting about the drawing of trumps.

# Try it Yourself

In each case you are declarer, sitting South. How should you play to give yourself the best possible chance to make your contract?

## Question 1

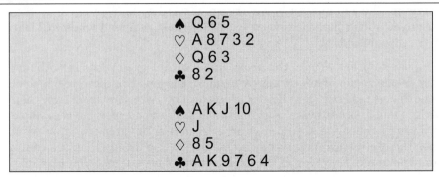

♠ Q 6 5
♡ A 8 7 3 2
◇ Q 6 3
♣ 8 2

♠ A K J 10
♡ J
◇ 8 5
♣ A K 9 7 6 4

| West | North | East | South |
|------|-------|------|-------|
|      |       |      | 1♣ |
| Pass | 1♡ | Pass | 1♠ |
| Pass | 1NT | Pass | 3♣ |
| Pass | 3♠ | Pass | 4♠ |
| All Pass |   |      |       |

West leads the ace of diamonds and a low diamond to the queen and king. East continues with the jack of diamonds.

## Question 2

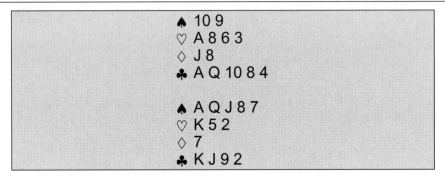

♠ 10 9
♡ A 8 6 3
◇ J 8
♣ A Q 10 8 4

♠ A Q J 8 7
♡ K 5 2
◇ 7
♣ K J 9 2

| West | North | East | South |
|------|-------|------|-------|
|      |       |      | 1♠ |
| Pass | 2♣ | Pass | 3♣ |
| Pass | 3♡ | Pass | 3♠ |
| Pass | 4♠ | All Pass |  |

West leads the king then queen of diamonds.

## Question 3

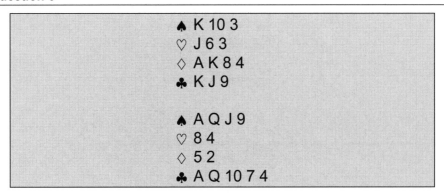

♠ K 10 3
♡ J 6 3
◇ A K 8 4
♣ K J 9

♠ A Q J 9
♡ 8 4
◇ 5 2
♣ A Q 10 7 4

| West | North | East | South |
|------|-------|------|-------|
|      |       |      | 1♣ |
| Pass | 1◇ | Pass | 1♠ |
| Pass | 2♡ | Pass | 3♣ |
| Pass | 3♠ | Pass | 4♠ |
| All Pass | | | |

West leads ace, king and a third heart to the queen.

## Question 4

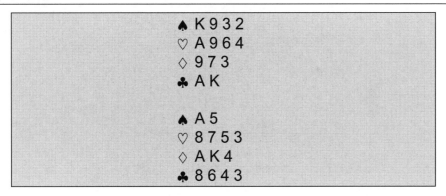

♠ K 9 3 2
♡ A 9 6 4
◇ 9 7 3
♣ A K

♠ A 5
♡ 8 7 5 3
◇ A K 4
♣ 8 6 4 3

| West | North | East | South |
|------|-------|------|-------|
|      | 1♣ (i) | Pass | 1♡ |
| Pass | 2♡ | Pass | 2NT |
| Pass | 4♡ | All Pass | |

(i) Playing 5-card majors and a prepared club

The queen of diamonds is led against Four Hearts.

## Question 5

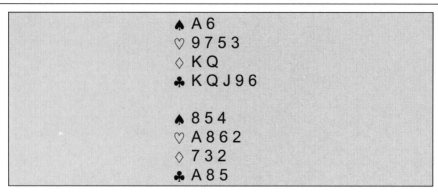

♠ A 6
♡ 9 7 5 3
◇ K Q
♣ K Q J 9 6

♠ 8 5 4
♡ A 8 6 2
◇ 7 3 2
♣ A 8 5

| West | North | East | South |
|------|-------|------|-------|
|      | 1♣    | Pass | 1♡    |
| Pass | 2♡    | All Pass |   |

West leads the jack of spades.

## Question 6

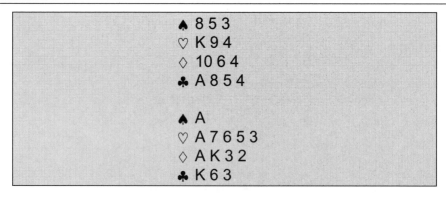

♠ 8 5 3
♡ K 9 4
◇ 10 6 4
♣ A 8 5 4

♠ A
♡ A 7 6 5 3
◇ A K 3 2
♣ K 6 3

| West | North | East | South |
|------|-------|------|-------|
|      |       |      | 1♡    |
| Pass | 2♡    | Pass | 4♡    |
| All Pass |   |      |       |

West leads a low spade.

## Question 7

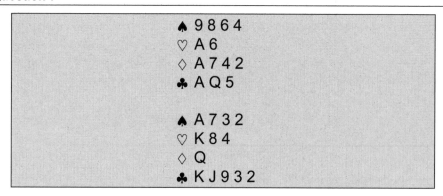

♠ 9 8 6 4
♡ A 6
◇ A 7 4 2
♣ A Q 5

♠ A 7 3 2
♡ K 8 4
◇ Q
♣ K J 9 3 2

| West | North | East | South |
|------|-------|------|-------|
|      |       |      | 1♣    |
| Pass | 1◇    | Pass | 1♠    |
| Pass | 4♠    | All Pass |   |

West leads the eight of diamonds to dummy's ace. Play on.

## Question 8

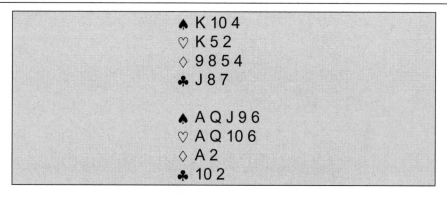

♠ K 10 4
♡ K 5 2
◇ 9 8 5 4
♣ J 8 7

♠ A Q J 9 6
♡ A Q 10 6
◇ A 2
♣ 10 2

| West | North | East | South |
|------|-------|------|-------|
|      |       |      | 1♠    |
| Pass | 2♠    | Pass | 4♠    |
| All Pass |   |      |       |

West leads the queen of diamonds.

## Question 9

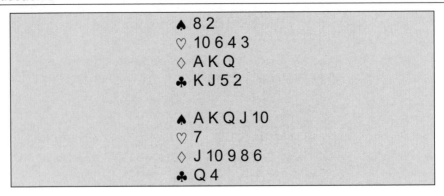

|       | ♠ 8 2          |
|-------|----------------|
|       | ♡ 10 6 4 3     |
|       | ◇ A K Q        |
|       | ♣ K J 5 2      |
|       |                |
|       | ♠ A K Q J 10   |
|       | ♡ 7            |
|       | ◇ J 10 9 8 6   |
|       | ♣ Q 4          |

| West | North | East | South |
|------|-------|------|-------|
|      |       |      | 1♠    |
| Pass | 2♣    | Pass | 2◇    |
| Pass | 2♡    | Pass | 2♠    |
| Pass | 3◇    | Pass | 3♠    |
| Pass | 4♠    | All Pass |    |

West leads the ace then queen of hearts.

## Question 10

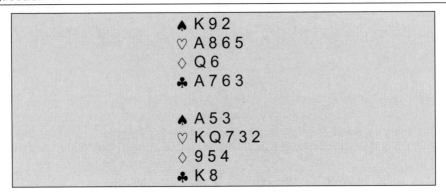

|       | ♠ K 9 2       |
|-------|---------------|
|       | ♡ A 8 6 5     |
|       | ◇ Q 6         |
|       | ♣ A 7 6 3     |
|       |               |
|       | ♠ A 5 3       |
|       | ♡ K Q 7 3 2   |
|       | ◇ 9 5 4       |
|       | ♣ K 8         |

| West | North | East | South |
|------|-------|------|-------|
|      |       |      | 1♡    |
| 2◇   | 4♡    | All Pass |    |

West leads ace, king and jack of diamonds, East playing high-low.

# Solutions

## Question 1

Declarer has two problems – retaining trump control and establishing the clubs. The latter can be done only if the suit breaks three-two, as declarer will run into a fatal ruff on a four-one split. If declarer ruffs at trick three, he will need an even trump split also. However, pitch a small club at trick three and dummy can look after a fourth diamond should the defence choose that line. More likely East switches to a heart. Win the ace and play three rounds of clubs, ruffing with the queen. Now draw trumps and succeed on any four-two or better split.

## Question 2

Discarding at trick two is not safe, as West may be able to switch to a club to set up a subsequent ruff. So declarer must ruff the second diamond. Crossing to dummy to take the trump finesse is not safe either. Say that West holds king to four trumps. He ducks the first round and, when you repeat the finesse, he wins and plays a diamond. A four-two trump break will lead to loss of control and eventual defeat. Try the effect of playing the spade queen from hand at trick three. Assuming that this holds the trick, cash the ace next and then leave trumps alone. Start playing winning clubs and let the defenders take their two remaining trumps whenever they wish.

## Question 3

This is a simple exercise in trump control. If declarer had a loser to throw on the third diamond it would be easy to see that it was correct to do so, as dummy can then take care of a fourth round of diamonds. Discarding retains trump control on four-two as well as three-three trump breaks. Well, if there are no losers, throw a winner. Trump control is crucial. Now declarer can win the next trick, draw trumps and claim ten tricks.

## Question 4

Declarer will need an even trump split if he is to succeed. He must play to ruff either two clubs in dummy or two spades in hand. There is a danger that the doubleton trump might over-ruff at some point, leaving four total losers, so declarer would like to draw two rounds of trumps before setting about his ruffs. Playing ace and another trump would run the risk of the defence winning the second trump and playing a third round, leaving only one trump in each hand with which to attempt to take two ruffs.

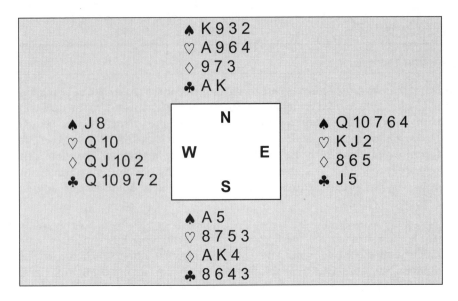

The solution is obvious once you think of it; declarer should win the opening lead and a duck a round of hearts, playing low from both hands. He wins the return and cashes the ace of hearts, then sets about taking his ruffs. Playing this way, the defence is restricted to two trump tricks whenever this is possible.

## Question 5

An optimist might win the ace of spades and play ace and another trump, thinking that as soon as trumps have been drawn he has an abundance of tricks in clubs. That would be a fatal error should the missing trumps be divided four-one, as the defender with the trump length would win the second round and draw all the rest of the trumps before cashing out the spades.

As on the previous deal, declarer should duck the first round of trumps to retain control. But before he even gets that far he should duck the opening lead to retain control of the dangerous side suit. Now he can win the continuation, duck a trump and win the return. After cashing the ace of trumps declarer can start rattling off the club winners and cannot be prevented from taking a spade ruff at some point for his eighth trick. Failure to duck at trick one could jeopardise that crucial ruff.

## Question 6

With a loser in each minor, declarer will need trumps to divide evenly. His tenth trick will have to come from one or other of the minor suits. A third club trick would require a three-three split, whereas diamonds could produce an extra trick either via an even split or a ruff of the fourth round in dummy.

Declarer cannot afford for the fourth diamond to be over-ruffed by the doubleton trump, so must draw two rounds of trumps before playing for the ruff. However, whichever way he tackles the trump suit, if he does so immediately there is a danger that the defence will play trumps back at him and prevent the ruff. So it is correct to play on diamonds first – but three rounds of that suit allows the defence to play the fourth round when the distribution is as feared. The solution? Play a low diamond from both hands at trick two. When declarer wins the next trick he can cash the top trumps and the top diamonds, eventually ruffing the fourth diamond if need be.

## Question 7

Does this look like just another case where declarer wins the opening lead then ducks a trump to retain control? This time a different technique is required. If declarer ducks a trump at trick two he is forced with a diamond. Now he cashes the ace of trumps as planned and discovers a four-one split so switches his attention to clubs. Alas, a defender ruffs, draws declarer's last trump and cashes a diamond or two.

The contract is quite secure on any four-one or three-two break. Simply cash the ace of trumps at trick two, then start on the clubs. The defence comes to three trump tricks but that is all.

## Question 8

Declarer's only problem appears to be the fourth heart. On a good day the suit will divide three-three, but when is it ever a good day? There is only one other possibility, and that is to try to ruff the fourth heart in dummy if the suit splits four-two.

Declarer wins the first diamond because there is no benefit to doing otherwise, then cashes the ace and king of trumps before playing on hearts. If the suit divides three-three, or if the same defender holds four hearts and three spades, then the fourth heart can indeed be ruffed in dummy. If a defender ruffs one of the winning hearts, then the suit was not splitting and the contract was doomed to failure anyway.

## Question 9

There is no point in discarding as the defence will just continue to lead hearts until declarer does finally ruff. There are ten winners but there is an awkward blockage, which may make cashing them a little tricky. If spades are four-two declarer will have to use all his trumps to draw them. If he then unblocks the diamonds he will have no quick entry back to hand to cash the last two diamonds and the defence will surely have sufficient winners to defeat the contract.

The key to success is to spot that declarer's own diamonds are solid so that dummy's honours are not actually required. If declarer ruffs the second heart and cashes just one diamond, he can then discard the two remaining diamond honours from dummy on the run of his four remaining trumps. Given a four-two or better trump break, declarer can now cash out the diamonds. Note that he can never risk a club play, as the defence can win and force him to ruff another heart.

## Question 10

A low ruff will surely see East over-ruff for the third defensive trick, and there is still a spade to lose for down one. Declarer may then be tempted to ruff with dummy's ace, but now he requires a two-two split or will again have a trump loser and four in all. The solution is not to ruff at all.

Declarer's best play is to swap the diamond ruff in dummy for a later spade ruff. He throws a spade at trick three and is in control barring a four-zero trump split, or a rather unlikely position where East has a singleton trump with which to ruff a fourth round of diamonds, thereby promoting a trump trick for his partner, which would always have been fatal whatever declarer tried. If West leads a fourth diamond, declarer can ruff or, if need be, over-ruff in hand, then draw trumps and take his spade ruff in dummy. Likewise, he wins any switch at trick three, draws trumps and ruffs his third spade for the tenth trick.

# Chapter Three

# Suit Establishment and Communications

♡ **Extra Tricks**

♡ **Maintaining Flexibility**

♡ **Points to Remember**

♡ **Try it Yourself**

 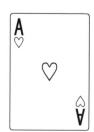 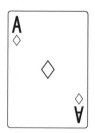 

# Extra Tricks

One of the benefits we get from having a trump suit is the possibility that we can establish extra length tricks in a side suit by ruffing. Holding, for example, K2 facing A8764, in a suit, it would usually be possible to create extra tricks even if playing in no-trumps, but that would involve losing one or more tricks in the suit. However, if this is a side suit and declarer has an ample trump fit and communications between the two hands, he may be able to establish one or two extra length tricks by ruffing, without having to give a trick to the defence along the way.

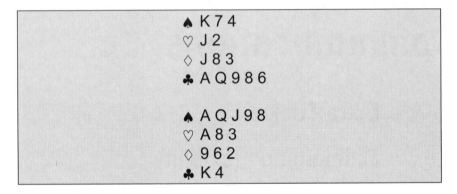

♠ K 7 4
♡ J 2
♢ J 8 3
♣ A Q 9 8 6

♠ A Q J 9 8
♡ A 8 3
♢ 9 6 2
♣ K 4

The contract is Four Spades and the lead is the king of hearts. Declarer has nine top tricks and a tenth could come by way of a heart ruff in the dummy. Unfortunately, there is a big danger that the defence will take three diamond tricks when they win their heart trick, leading to one down. One possible solution would be for declarer to try to cash three rounds of clubs to discard a diamond before he gave up the heart trick but, of course, the third round of clubs would stand up only if the suit splits evenly, in which case simply drawing trumps and cashing the clubs would lead to eleven easy tricks. The even club split will occur only a little over one time in three. However, a four-two or better split is a very good chance, which suggests a better line of play.

Declarer should win the opening lead for fear of a deadly diamond switch. Now he cashes the ace and queen of spades. If the suit splits four-one he will have to just draw the rest of the trumps and then play for a three-three club split. But if spades divide three-two, declarer next plays king of clubs, a club to the ace, and ruffs a club with the jack of spades. That will establish a fourth club winner, and he can now cross to dummy with the carefully preserved king of trumps to cash the clubs, coming to ten tricks.

This next example requires a little more work on declarer's part.

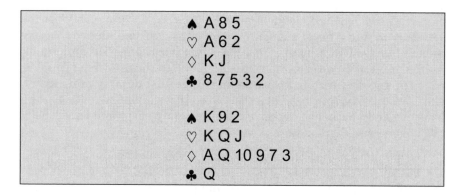

♠ A 8 5
♡ A 6 2
♦ K J
♣ 8 7 5 3 2

♠ K 9 2
♡ K Q J
♦ A Q 10 9 7 3
♣ Q

A spade is led against Six Diamonds. There is an inescapable club loser and only one possible resting place for declarer's third spade. It may look to be a long way off, but declarer must play to establish the fifth club for a spade discard. He will have to watch his entries to dummy, so should set about establishing his club trick immediately. Win the opening spade lead in hand and lead the queen of clubs. Say that whoever wins the club returns a spade to dummy's ace. Ruff a club, cross to the jack of diamonds and ruff another club. Now play a diamond to the king and ruff the fourth club. If everything has passed off peacefully, declarer can now draw the last trump and cross to dummy's ace of hearts to cash the established club. It needs both minors to divide evenly but that is all, provided that declarer has not wasted any of his dummy entries.

Suit establishment and communications are two concepts that are irrevocably intertwined. Try this next one.

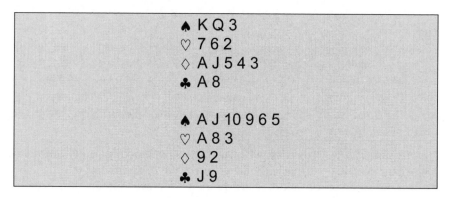

♠ K Q 3
♡ 7 6 2
♦ A J 5 4 3
♣ A 8

♠ A J 10 9 6 5
♡ A 8 3
♦ 9 2
♣ J 9

West leads the king of clubs against Four Spades. Declarer can see nine top tricks so needs just one more, which will presumably have to come from diamonds. The king and queen of diamonds could both be onside, but that is a poor chance. Careful play will establish an extra diamond trick whenever the suit splits either three-three or four-two.

Declarer wins the opening lead because he does not wish to give West the opportunity to find a heart switch. Now he must duck a diamond, playing low from both hands. This is to preserve his communications with dummy. If he crossed to hand with a trump to lead a diamond to the jack, East could win and return a second trump, knocking an entry out of dummy prematurely. Declarer would find that he required a three-three diamond split. Likewise, playing ace and another diamond wastes a dummy entry and leaves declarer in need of an even diamond break.

Once the diamond is ducked, however, only a very bad spade or diamond break will defeat the contract. The defenders cash their club winner and switch to hearts. Declarer wins the ace and plays a diamond to the ace, then ruffs a diamond high. If they split three-three he draws trumps ending in dummy. If the diamonds were four-two, he crosses to the king of spades and ruffs another diamond high, after which he draws trumps ending in dummy and cashes the fifth diamond.

# Maintaining Flexibility

Sometimes, declarer must take a very flexible approach and make a play that looks to be very unnatural if he is to preserve his communications.

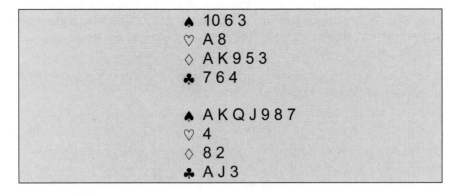

What is the most likely source of declarer's twelfth trick in Six Spades after the lead of the queen of hearts?

It is clear that the twelfth trick will have to be provided by the diamond suit. If declarer wins the opening lead, draws a couple of rounds of trumps, then plays three rounds of diamonds, ruffing, he will succeed if the suit breaks three-three. But a three-three break does not offer very good odds. There is a much stronger line which more than doubles the chances of success, but it requires a counter-intuitive play from declarer.

In a no-trump contract, it would be easy to see that ducking the first round of diamonds would help with the communications, but when this is a side suit in a trump contract, it looks strange when holding a doubleton opposite a suit headed by the ace and king. Nonetheless, the best play is to win the opening lead and duck a diamond at trick two. Any return can be won in declarer's hand. He draws a couple of rounds of trumps, being careful to leave the ten in dummy, then plays a diamond to the ace and ruffs a diamond. Finally, declarer crosses to the ten of spades and cashes two diamond winners, pitching his heart losers. The contract is made whenever diamonds break either three-three or four-two.

The key to good and effective suit establishment is always to take care of our communications. Always plan the play before setting out. If you think you have found a good play, in the last example perhaps playing ace, king and a third diamond to ruff, pause for a few moments to see if you can find an even better play, as in ducking the first diamond above.

# Points to Remember

♠ An adequate trump suit can allow side suits to be established to provide extra winners but declarer must always take care that he has the necessary communications to make this possible.

♠ Sometimes it is necessary to take a very flexible approach to the play, perhaps making a quite unnatural looking play to achieve the desired result. Do not make routine plays without thinking, rather, always bear in mind what you are trying to achieve.

♠ When you think you have found a good line of play, give it a little more thought to see if there is something even better available.

# Try it Yourself

In each case you are declarer, sitting South. How should you play to give yourself the best possible chance to make your contract?

### Question 1

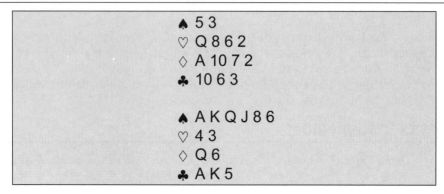

| West | North | East | South |
|------|-------|------|-------|
|      |       |      | 2♠ |
| Pass | 2NT | Pass | 3♠ |
| Pass | 4♠ | All Pass | |

West leads the two of clubs to the ten and jack. Play on.

### Question 2

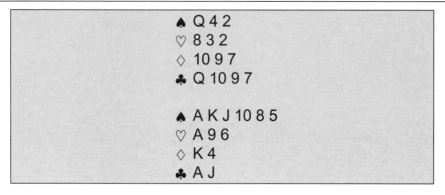

| West | North | East | South |
|------|-------|------|-------|
|      |       |      | 2♠ |
| Pass | 2NT | Pass | 3♠ |
| Pass | 4♠ | All Pass | |

West leads the six of clubs.

## Question 3

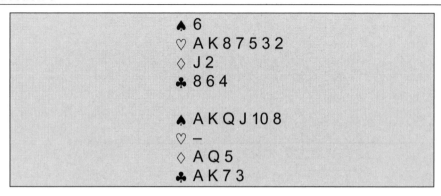

♠ 6
♡ A K 8 7 5 3 2
◇ J 2
♣ 8 6 4

♠ A K Q J 10 8
♡ —
◇ A Q 5
♣ A K 7 3

| West | North | East | South |
|------|-------|------|-------|
|      |       |      | 2♣    |
| Pass | 2♡    | Pass | 2♠    |
| Pass | 3♡    | Pass | 3♠    |
| Pass | 4♡    | Pass | 6♠    |
| All Pass |   |      |       |

The opening lead is the jack of clubs.

## Question 4

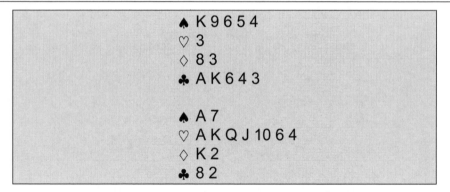

♠ K 9 6 5 4
♡ 3
◇ 8 3
♣ A K 6 4 3

♠ A 7
♡ A K Q J 10 6 4
◇ K 2
♣ 8 2

| West | North | East | South |
|------|-------|------|-------|
|      |       |      | 2♡    |
| Pass | 2♠    | Pass | 4♡    |
| Pass | 5♣ (i) | Pass | 5♠ (i) |
| Pass | 6♣ (i) | Pass | 6◇ (i) |
| Pass | 6♡    | All Pass |   |

(i) Cuebids

The opening lead is the seven of hearts.

**43**

## Question 5

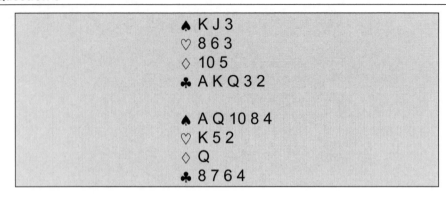

♠ K J 3
♡ 8 6 3
◇ 10 5
♣ A K Q 3 2

♠ A Q 10 8 4
♡ K 5 2
◇ Q
♣ 8 7 6 4

| West | North | East | South |
|------|-------|------|-------|
|      | 1♣    | Pass | 1♠    |
| 2◇   | 2♠    | 3◇   | 4♠    |
| All Pass | | | |

West leads the ace then king of diamonds.

## Question 6

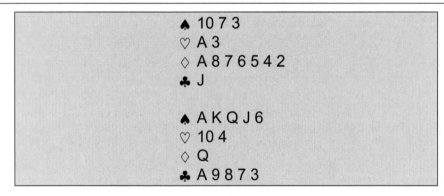

♠ 10 7 3
♡ A 3
◇ A 8 7 6 5 4 2
♣ J

♠ A K Q J 6
♡ 10 4
◇ Q
♣ A 9 8 7 3

| West | North | East | South |
|------|-------|------|-------|
|      | 1◇    | Pass | 1♠    |
| Pass | 2◇    | Pass | 3♣    |
| Pass | 4♠    | Pass | 5♣    |
| Pass | 5♡    | Pass | 6♠    |
| All Pass | | | |

West leads the four of clubs.

## Question 7

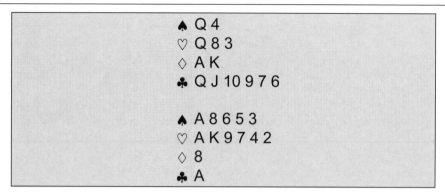

♠ Q 4
♡ Q 8 3
◇ A K
♣ Q J 10 9 7 6

♠ A 8 6 5 3
♡ A K 9 7 4 2
◇ 8
♣ A

| West | North | East | South |
|------|-------|------|-------|
|      |       |      | 1♡    |
| Pass | 2♣    | Pass | 2♠    |
| Pass | 3♡    | Pass | 3♠    |
| Pass | 4◇    | Pass | 6♡    |
| All Pass |   |      |       |

West leads the queen of diamonds.

## Question 8

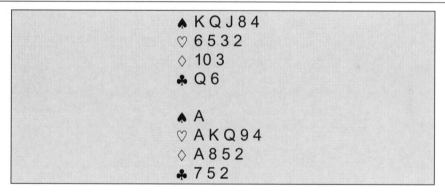

♠ K Q J 8 4
♡ 6 5 3 2
◇ 10 3
♣ Q 6

♠ A
♡ A K Q 9 4
◇ A 8 5 2
♣ 7 5 2

| West | North | East | South |
|------|-------|------|-------|
|      |       | Pass | 1♡    |
| 2♣   | 2♡    | Pass | 4♡    |
| All Pass |   |      |       |

West leads ace, king of clubs, East following three, eight. West continues clubs.

## Question 9

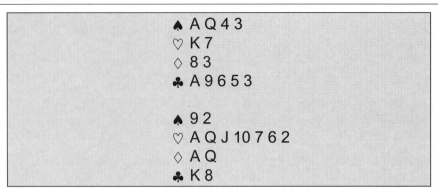

♠ A Q 4 3
♡ K 7
◇ 8 3
♣ A 9 6 5 3

♠ 9 2
♡ A Q J 10 7 6 2
◇ A Q
♣ K 8

| West | North | East | South |
|------|-------|------|-------|
|      |       |      | 2♡    |
| Pass | 3♣    | Pass | 3♡    |
| Pass | 4NT   | Pass | 5♡    |
| Pass | 6♡    | All Pass |    |

West leads the eight of spades.

## Question 10

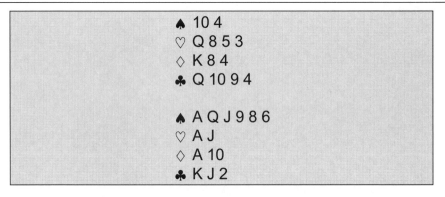

♠ 10 4
♡ Q 8 5 3
◇ K 8 4
♣ Q 10 9 4

♠ A Q J 9 8 6
♡ A J
◇ A 10
♣ K J 2

| West | North | East | South |
|------|-------|------|-------|
|      |       |      | 2♣    |
| Pass | 2NT   | Pass | 3♠    |
| Pass | 4♠    | Pass | 6♠    |
| All Pass |   |      |       |

The opening lead is the queen of diamonds.

# Solutions

## Question 1

Declarer has nine tricks and must find a tenth. Were both top heart honours onside, West would surely have led one, so leading twice towards the queen will not work. There is no scope in clubs, so the only hope is a second diamond winner. Normally, declarer would lead low to the queen, then perhaps finesse the ten if the queen lost to king. Here, there are no side entries to the dummy, so that play is not an option.

Declarer should win the club lead and draw trumps, then lead the queen of diamonds, ducking in dummy whether or not the king appears, as otherwise communications with the dummy have been cut. With the king and queen out of the way, the stage is set for a second-round finesse of the ten. The position of the diamond king is completely irrelevant to the success or failure of this contract; it is the position of the jack that is important, and declarer will succeed if it is in the West hand, as the second-round finesse will win.

## Question 2

The lead appears to have given declarer a free finesse. However, if he takes advantage of the 'free' gift by winning with the jack, the contract will then depend on a favourably placed ace of diamonds. Declarer wins the club, draws trumps and has to try a diamond to the king, as he has only two club tricks.

Now try it again if declarer wins the club ace at trick one even though the king has not appeared. He cashes the ace and king of trumps, then plays the club jack, overtaking with the queen. It does the defence no good to duck this trick, as a third club is played to knock out the king. Declarer still has a dummy entry with the queen of spades and can cash the established clubs, making in all six spades, three clubs and a heart. This line is not quite secure, but makes the hand whenever it can be made.

## Question 3

There are twelve tricks but two of those are the ace and king of hearts, currently stranded in dummy. There is a neat way to force an entry to the dummy. Ace and another diamond sees the jack lose to the king and a trump is returned; no good. Likewise, a low diamond from hand is also taken by the king, and again a trump is returned. But try the effect of winning the opening lead and playing the diamond queen from hand. If the king is taken, the jack will be an entry to the heart winners, while if the diamond is ducked declarer can continue with ace and a third diamond, ruffed in dummy. Given reasonable breaks, there is no escape for the defence.

## Question 4

Declarer draws trumps and has to decide which of dummy's suits he should attempt to establish to provide a twelfth trick without being reliant on the position of the ace of diamonds. It is correct to play to establish the spades because the ace and king of clubs will then provide entries to dummy. If declarer tries to set up the clubs, there is only one outside entry, the spade king. The difference is that spades can be established and cashed on either a three-three or four-two split, whereas playing on clubs will be successful only if the suit breaks three-three. If the chosen suit fails to deliver, declarer has to fall back on a diamond to the king.

## Question 5

There appear to be ten easy tricks, five in each black suit. But wait, if the clubs are three-one there is an awkward blockage. Declarer cannot afford to duck a club, in case the ace of hearts is offside. So if declarer ruffs at trick two then draws trumps, he is dependent on an even club split. The solution is simply to discard a club on the second diamond. That gets rid of the blockage and declarer can draw trumps as soon as he gains the lead, then run the clubs even if they do split three-one.

## Question 6

There are insufficient trumps between the two hands to attempt to ruff out the clubs and cash the long card after drawing trumps. The best prospect of success is to establish dummy's diamonds, but entries to dummy are at a premium. Declarer wins the opening lead and plays ace of diamonds and ruffs a diamond high. Then he crosses to the ace of hearts and ruffs another diamond high. Now he can draw trumps ending with dummy's queen and, hopefully, cash the established diamonds.

This line will succeed if both key suits split three-two. The crucial play is that both diamond ruffs must be taken with high trumps, allowing the last trump to be drawn while crossing to dummy's ten. Otherwise, dummy is an entry short.

## Question 7

Declarer can succeed against either a two-two or three-one trump split if he can establish a side suit for the loss of only one trick. A spade to the queen, followed by a spade ruff in dummy, may prove to be successful, but a four-two break puts the contract in serious jeopardy. Better is to play to establish the clubs, but there is an awkward blockage. Say that trumps are three-one and declarer unblocks the club ace, then plays two rounds of trumps ending in dummy. He can establish the clubs with the aid of the ruffing finesse, but how will he get back to the winners?

The problem is that declarer's clubs are too good – the play would be easy to see if his own club was a low card. Correct play is to win the opening lead and cash the second diamond, throwing the blocking ace of clubs away. Now take and, if necessary, repeat the ruffing club finesse. The suit can be established on reasonable breaks and trumps drawn ending in dummy to cash the established winners.

## Question 8

If declarer ruffs the third club in dummy he will have no sure way to get to dummy again after unblocking the spades. He will be OK if trumps split two-two but three-one is more likely. The solution is to discard a diamond at trick three. Declarer can now win any return and cash the top trumps and ace of spades before crossing to dummy with a diamond ruff to enjoy the spade winners.

## Question 9

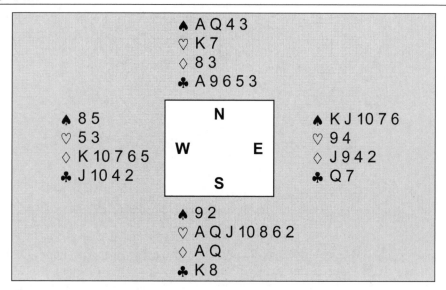

The lead suggests that the spade finesse will fail, leaving declarer dependent on either a successful diamond finesse or being able to establish and cash the clubs. The latter is the better prospect, as careful play allows declarer to succeed on either a three-three or four-two club split. But to make that possible he must watch his dummy entries.

Say that declarer finesses the spade queen at trick one. It loses and a spade is returned, knocking out the ace. Declarer plays three rounds of clubs, ruffing, then ace and another trump. Though trumps are drawn, the clubs have not been established and there are no more dummy entries, leaving the fate of the contract hanging on the diamond finesse.

Rising with the ace at trick one is no better. Again, declarer can try three rounds of clubs, but again the king of hearts is the sole remaining dummy entry and the clubs are not yet set up.

The solution is to play low from dummy at trick one. East will win the trick but, unless the spades are six-one, can do nothing to hurt declarer. Most likely East will switch to a diamond. Declarer takes the ace and plays three rounds of clubs, ruffing high. Two rounds of trumps ending in dummy allows a second club ruff, after which declarer can draw any outstanding trumps. Finally, he can cross to the carefully preserved ace of spades and cash the long club, his twelfth trick.

## Question 10

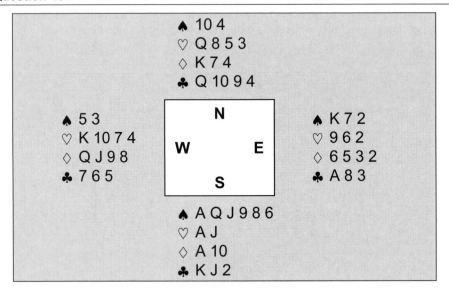

Declarer has bid very aggressively and the contract is not a good one. Looking at a sure club loser, declarer will need to bring in the trumps without loss, presumably via the finesse. He may be tempted therefore to win the diamond in dummy and run the ten of spades. Good news; East turns up with the king of spades and it is captured by a second finesse. Declarer draws the last trump and plays the king followed by the jack of clubs, but the ace is ducked twice. The best that declarer can now do is to overtake the second club in dummy and fall back on the heart finesse. Unlucky!

Or was it unlucky? Declarer used his one sure late dummy entry prematurely. Better is to win the opening lead in hand with the ace and lead the jack of clubs to the queen. If the ace is ducked, declarer is in dummy to take the trump finesse. After drawing trumps he reverts to clubs, and the king of diamonds is still there as an entry to the fourth club. If the defence takes the first club, declarer wins the return and crosses to the diamond king to take the trump finesse. After drawing trumps the clubs themselves provide an entry to the extra winner. In either case, there is no need for the heart finesse.

# Chapter Four

# Suit Combinations and Safety Plays

♡ **Playing the Odds**

♡ **Considering the Whole Hand**

♡ **Points to Remember**

♡ **Try it Yourself**

 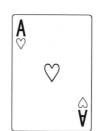 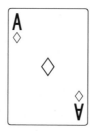 

# Playing the Odds

While declarer should play the whole hand and not just one suit in isolation, it does pay to know what the correct 'odds' plays are with various common suit combinations. I cannot stress too strongly, however, that I am now discussing only the theoretically correct plays in isolation, and that these should sometimes be deviated from to cater to any special problems that may be created by the rest of the hand.

We all know that it is correct to play for the drop, cashing the ace and king, if holding nine cards missing the queen. Equally, if holding only eight cards missing the queen, it is normally correct to cash one top honour then finesse on the next round. However, even that last one assumes that we can then repeat the finesse if need be.

**(i)  A K J 10 8 7 facing   3 2**

It is correct to finesse the jack on the first round, without first cashing the ace or king. Yes, this risks losing to bare queen offside, but it gains whenever there is any other singleton offside, i.e. there is queen to four onside, which is four times as likely. Cashing the ace first would make it impossible to pick up queen to four as it is possible to take only one finesse.

**(ii)  J 10 9 8     facing   A 7 6 5 4**

Correct play, though it is quite close, is to take two finesses. Of the times that success is possible, declarer loses only to king, queen doubleton offside.

**(iii) A Q 9 2     facing   5 4 3**

If declarer can afford a loser in this suit, correct play is to lead low to the nine first before trying the simple finesse of the queen, which he can try on the second round. This gains when South holds both jack and ten.

**(iv) A K 10 3 2    facing   Q 9 5 4**

Cashing one of the ace and king first allows declarer to pick up jack to four with either opponent. But beware that similar holdings are not necessarily identical so:

**(v)  A K 8 3 2    facing   Q 9 5 4**

Jack, ten to four can be picked up without loss only if it is South who holds the four cards, as it is only West who has two cards bigger than the two missing honours. But this is achieved only if declarer starts by cashing the queen.

**(vi) K J 3 2     facing   A 9 5 4**

If needing all four tricks from this suit, it is correct to lead low to the jack on the first round. Cashing the ace first prevents an unfortunate loss to the bare queen in the North hand, but when that is the layout there is no way to come to four tricks. Leading low towards the jack gains when it is South who holds the bare queen, as the king wins, the jack is cashed and the nine finessed on the third round.

Now suppose that only three tricks are required and a loser is acceptable to declarer. There is a sure line with this combination, but it might be tough to work it out if you hadn't seen it before. Correct technique is to cash the king first and then lead low, intending to put in the nine if North plays the remaining small card. The point is that if South can beat the nine then the suit must have broken three-two and declarer will have his three tricks, while if the nine scores that also provides the third winner. If North plays an honour, declarer wins the ace and can easily create a third winner, while if North shows out, declarer hops up with the ace and leads towards the jack, again ensuring a third trick.

## Considering the Whole Hand

Once again, it is important to look at the whole hand and consider what is actually needed to bring success. Take this example:

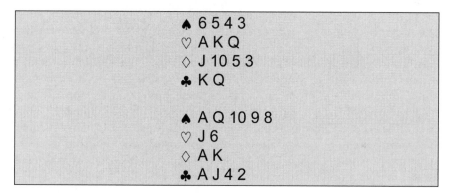

The contract is Seven Spades on the lead of the eight of hearts. Somebody has overbid; this is not a good contract. Declarer must bring in the trump suit without loss. The best chance is to lead low to the queen. This will succeed when East holds king doubleton or when West has the bare jack, as that will fall under the queen and declarer can cross back to dummy to finesse the ten next.

Now suppose that the contract is only Six Spades. Prospects are rather better. But the play that was correct in a grand slam would be a poor effort when playing the small slam. If the finesse of the queen lost to the king, declarer would then have to guess whether to next lay down the ace or to finesse the ten. Unless both missing honours are guarded offside, the contract is virtually secure, but not if declarer takes any first-round finesse. Instead, he should lay down the ace, thereby catching any bare honours offside. If only small cards appear he crosses to dummy and leads towards his hand. Even king, jack to four with East can be picked up this way.

Now suppose that the contract is still Six Spades but we turn the ace of clubs into a small card. Now there is a sure loser outside the trump suit and we are back to the situation where trumps must be played without loss. As we have seen, that means leading low to the queen on the first round.

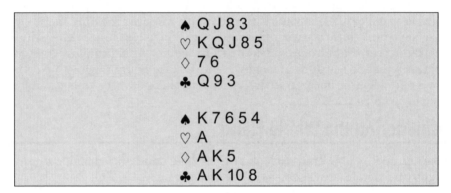

In the previous example declarer needed to be optimistic and pray for luck in his trump suit. This time he needs to be pessimistic and assume the worst. The only thing which is likely to defeat Six Spades after a diamond lead is a four-zero trump split. It would be all too easy for declarer to win the opening lead and follow with a low trump to the queen. Easy, but incorrect. The contract is secure on all three-one or two-two breaks. If East holds ♠ A1092, he cannot be prevented from making two tricks in the suit. But if West has the same holding it can be picked up for only one loser, provided that declarer's first trump play is the king. That forces the ace, and now a double finesse against ten and nine brings home the contract.

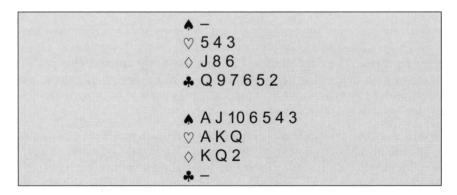

Declarer is in Four Spades on the lead of the jack of hearts. This type of trump holding is misplayed time and time again in clubs up and down the land. Declarers play ace then jack of spades, sometimes creating a third loser for themselves where they should have escaped with only two, which is the whole point of the hand, of course. Correct play is to win the opening lead then play ace followed by a low trump. If the suit breaks three-three then it will not matter what play is tried. If a defender holds king, queen to four, he will always make three tricks, whatever declarer does. But where one defender holds honour doubleton and the other honour to four, the play of ace and a low card will see the doubleton honour fall on thin air. Now declarer can lead the jack or ten to knock out the remaining honour and not have to lose a trick to any of the small cards.

There are many suit combinations like that last one which are obvious when you stop to think about them. The problems come when declarer plays too quickly.

## Points to Remember

♠ It is helpful to know the correct odds plays when holding different suit combinations.

♠ Do not play suits in isolation. Sometimes the requirements of the whole hand suggest that the normal odds play may not be correct on a particular deal.

♠ Do not make the mistake of thinking that similar suit combinations should necessarily be played identically.

♠ Identical suit combinations may be played in different fashions according to the number of winners required or losers that can be afforded in the suit.

# Try it Yourself

In each case you are declarer, sitting South. How should you play to give yourself the best possible chance to make your contract?

## Question 1

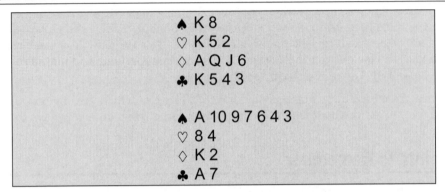

♠ K 8
♡ K 5 2
◊ A Q J 6
♣ K 5 4 3

♠ A 10 9 7 6 4 3
♡ 8 4
◊ K 2
♣ A 7

| West | North | East | South |
|------|-------|------|-------|
|      | 1NT   | Pass | 3♠    |
| Pass | 3NT   | Pass | 4♠    |
| All Pass |   |      |       |

West leads the queen of hearts to the king and ace. Back comes a second heart to the ten, followed by the heart jack.

## Question 2

♠ 7 6 3
♡ 7
◊ A 7 5 4 2
♣ J 8 6 4

♠ A K Q
♡ K Q 10 6 5 4 2
◊ 9
♣ A 3

| West | North | East | South |
|------|-------|------|-------|
|      |       |      | 2♡    |
| Pass | 2NT   | Pass | 3♡    |
| Pass | 3NT   | Pass | 4♡    |
| All Pass |   |      |       |

West leads the queen of diamonds.

## Question 3

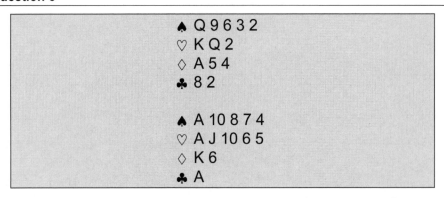

| West | North | East | South |
|------|-------|------|-------|
|      |       |      | 1♠    |
| Pass | 4♠    | Pass | 6♠    |
| All Pass |   |      |       |

The opening lead is the king of clubs.

## Question 4

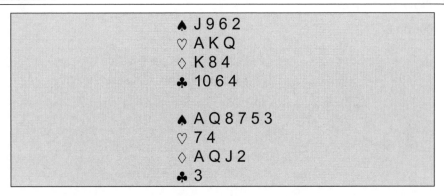

| West | North | East | South |
|------|-------|------|-------|
|      |       |      | 1♠    |
| Pass | 4◇ (i) | Pass | 4NT   |
| Pass | 5◇    | Pass | 6♠    |
| All Pass |   |      |       |

(i) Good raise to 4♠

West leads the king then queen of clubs.

## Question 5

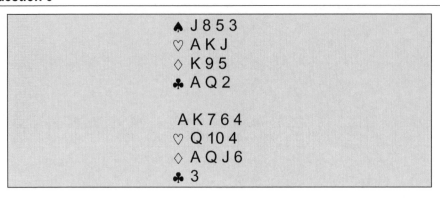

♠ J 8 5 3
♡ A K J
◇ K 9 5
♣ A Q 2

A K 7 6 4
♡ Q 10 4
◇ A Q J 6
♣ 3

| West | North | East | South |
|------|-------|------|-------|
|      |       |      | 1♠    |
| Pass | 2♣    | Pass | 3◇    |
| Pass | 4NT   | Pass | 5♡    |
| Pass | 5NT   | Pass | 6◇    |
| Pass | 6♠    | All Pass |    |

West leads the jack of clubs.

## Question 6

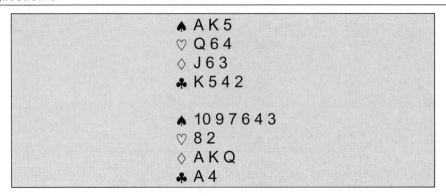

♠ A K 5
♡ Q 6 4
◇ J 6 3
♣ K 5 4 2

♠ 10 9 7 6 4 3
♡ 8 2
◇ A K Q
♣ A 4

| West | North | East | South |
|------|-------|------|-------|
|      |       |      | 1♠    |
| Pass | 3NT   | Pass | 4♠    |
| All Pass |   |      |       |

West leads a low heart to the jack. East cashes the heart ace, then plays a low heart.

## Question 7

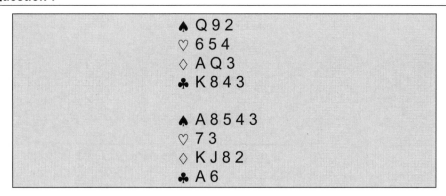

♠ Q 9 2
♡ 6 5 4
♢ A Q 3
♣ K 8 4 3

♠ A 8 5 4 3
♡ 7 3
♢ K J 8 2
♣ A 6

| West | North | East | South |
|------|-------|------|-------|
|      |       | 1NT(i) | 2♠ |
| Pass | 4♠ | All Pass | |

(i) 16-18

West leads the ten of hearts to East's jack. East continues with the ace then king of hearts.

## Question 8

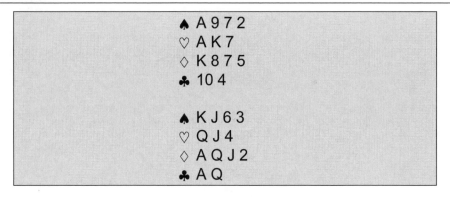

♠ A 9 7 2
♡ A K 7
♢ K 8 7 5
♣ 10 4

♠ K J 6 3
♡ Q J 4
♢ A Q J 2
♣ A Q

| West | North | East | South |
|------|-------|------|-------|
|      | 1♢ | Pass | 1♠ |
| Pass | 2♠ | Pass | 4NT |
| Pass | 5♡ | Pass | 5NT |
| Pass | 6♡ | Pass | 6♠ |
| All Pass | | | |

The opening lead is the five of hearts.

## Question 9

♠ Q 7 4 3
♡ 8 6
◇ K Q 8 2
♣ A K 5

♠ A J 8 6 5
♡ Q 4 3
◇ J 10 9 7 4
♣ —

| West | North | East | South |
|------|-------|------|-------|
|      |       | 1NT(i) | 2♠ |
| Pass | 4♠ | All Pass | |

(i) 16-18

West leads the jack of hearts to East's king. East cashes the heart ace, then switches to ace and another diamond, West following both times. Play on.

## Question 10

♠ 7 5 4
♡ A 2
◇ Q J 10 9 5
♣ 8 4 2

♠ A K J 10 9 6 3
♡ 8
◇ A K
♣ A Q J

| West | North | East | South |
|------|-------|------|-------|
|      |       |      | 2♣ |
| Pass | 2◇ | Pass | 2♠ |
| Pass | 3♠ | Pass | 4♣ |
| Pass | 4♡ | Pass | 6♠ |
| All Pass | | | |

The opening lead is the king of hearts.

# Solutions

## Question 1

Declarer's only problem is to avoid losing two trump tricks, and there can be two losers only if the suit breaks four-zero. Ruffing the third heart and leading to the king of spades will be good enough if it is East who holds all four trumps, but it will lead to defeat if West has them all. There is a perfect safety play, namely to lead a low spade to dummy's eight. If West does hold all four trumps, the eight will win and there will be only one loser; while if the eight loses to East, the suit cannot break worse than three-one and the remainder will fall under the king and ace.

## Question 2

Declarer has one inescapable club loser and must hold his trump losers to two. It must be correct to win dummy's ace of diamonds to lead a heart towards the honours in hand in case East holds the bare ace. In practice, East plays low. Any play should succeed on a three-two trump break, but what if they are four-one with East holding the length? The odds favour finessing the ten. This will cost if West holds the bare jack, but will gain when he has the bare ace or a small singleton, considerably more likely. The king can be played on the second round, followed by the queen.

## Question 3

There are no losers outside the trump suit, but a misplay could result in two losers there if the same defender holds all three cards. The main trap to avoid is laying down the ace of trumps, which would lose out to KJx with East. Instead, either lead low from hand or cross to dummy's ace of diamonds and lead a low card, covering as cheaply as possible the card played by East. Now there is no way to lose more than one trick.

## Question 4

After ruffing the second club, there is only one problem. Declarer must play the trumps without loss. It is correct to finesse, but a careless player might cross to dummy then lead low to the queen. If East holds all three missing trumps this will leave him with a third-round winner. Correct play is to cross to dummy and lead the jack of spades for the finesse. If East does hold K10x, this will show up on the first round; declarer can then win the king with the ace and cross back to dummy to finesse against the ten.

## Question 5

Once again, the only possible problem is the trump suit. Nine players out of ten would win the ace of clubs and lay down the ace of trumps. And nine players out of ten would be wrong to do so. The play of a top trump costs the contract when East has all four missing trumps. Instead, lead low from the dummy at trick two and, if East follows, just cover his card. Declarer's combined trump spots are sufficient to ensure only one loser via repeated finesses if need be. If East shows out on the first trump, then ace, king and a third round towards the jack will pick up West's queen to four for only one loser.

## Question 6

Declarer ruffs the third heart and must decide how to play the trump suit. As on the previous deal, many players would just cash the ace and look disappointed if East showed out, leaving West with two trump tricks. If East has all four trumps then nothing can be done, but there is a safety play to cater to all four cards being with West. At trick four, lead the ten of spades and, if West plays low, run it. If this card loses to East there are only two trumps outstanding and these can be drawn by the ace and king. Declarer must remember to ruff a heart return in hand to preserve the top trumps in dummy. If West covers the spade win and, if East shows out, cross to the ace of clubs to lead the spade nine next. The trump spots are sufficiently good to restrict West to only one trump trick.

## Question 7

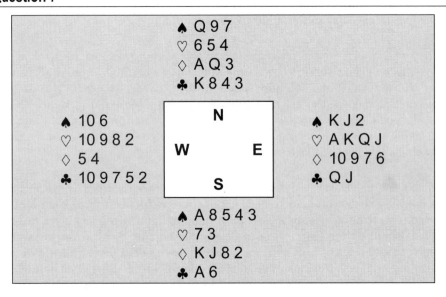

Declarer ruffs the third heart. The auction tells him that the king of spades is sitting over the queen. That leaves the simple play of ace and a low spade, ducking in dummy and hoping to drop a doubleton king, or the considerably more exotic technique known as an intra-finesse. Before committing himself to a trump play, declarer should see if he can discover more about the opposing distribution. The only side suit that he can afford to play more than two rounds of is clubs, as there may be a ruff if he leads too many rounds of diamonds. He leads ace of clubs, a club to the king and ruffs a club. If everyone follows, perhaps he settles for the simple spade play as described above. But in practice East discards on the third club. As it would be unusual to open One No-trump with two doubletons, East is unlikely to hold king doubleton spade. There is only one other chance.

Declarer continues by leading a low spade to the nine and jack. He wins the diamond return in dummy and leads the spade queen. If the cards are as he hopes, this fetches the king from East and pins the ten in the West hand. This is an intra-finesse, a name coined by Brazilian star Gabriel Chagas, who first played this deal. Of course, the play is equally successful if the ten and jack of spades are switched.

## Question 8

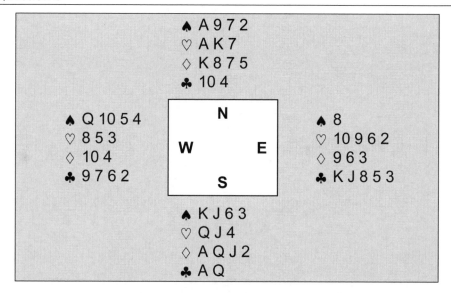

The key will be the spade suit. There are two different ways in which to play this combination, according to the number of tricks required.

If declarer requires all four tricks with no loser, the correct play is low to the jack on the first round. This is better than cashing the ace first because it caters to bare queen with East. Cashing the ace first prevents the loss of a trick to bare queen with West, but then four winners were impossible anyway.

If declarer can afford one trump loser but not two, the correct play is to start by cashing the king and then lead low, intending to put in dummy's nine if West plays low. Of course, were West to show out, declarer would hop up with the ace and lead back through East's queen to hold him to one winner. This is a 100% guaranteed safety play assuming the suit to be no worse than four-one.

Here, declarer does not know how many losers he can afford until he has taken the club finesse. If it wins, he takes the safety play; if it loses he goes all out for four spade tricks.

## Question 9

Normal play in the trump suit is to lead low to the jack, but that is to cater to the possibility of bare king with East, which is not possible this time. East has opened One No-trump and turned up with one doubleton already, so rates to hold at least three spades. That looks ominous, but declarer can still prevail if West has the bare nine or ten. Win the second diamond in dummy and lead the queen of trumps to the king and ace. If the nine or ten drops, cross back to dummy by ruffing the winning queen of hearts and finesse the spade eight.

## Question 10

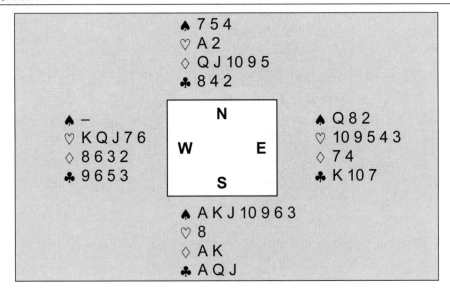

| West | North | East | South |
|------|-------|------|-------|
|      |       |      | 2♣    |
| Pass | 2◇    | Pass | 2♠    |
| Pass | 3♠    | Pass | 4♣    |
| Pass | 4♡    | Pass | 6♠    |
| All Pass |   |      |       |

The opening lead is the king of hearts.

After winning the ace of hearts, the percentage play in the trump suit is, of course, to lay down the ace. However, that is looking at the suit in isolation. If declarer plays a spade to the ace at trick two and finds East with queen to three trumps, he will go down, as there is no entry to the dummy and there is a club loser and a spade loser.

A spade to the jack at trick two ensures the contract (provided that East follows; if East is void, the contract always fails unless there is a singleton king of clubs). If the finesse wins, there is no trump loser and declarer can just give up a club after drawing trumps. If the finesse loses, declarer can win the return, cash a top spade to draw the one remaining defensive trump, and unblock the ace and king of diamonds. The spade seven is an entry to the diamond winners, and there is no need to concede a club trick.

**Chapter Five**

---

# Knowing the Odds and Combining Chances

♡ **Basic Odds**

♡ **Combining Chances**

♡ **Points to Remember**

♡ **Try it Yourself**

  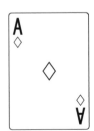 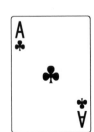

# Basic Odds

It is not necessary to know all the odds on various suit combinations being played successfully, but it helps to be aware of the most common odds. As a general rule, if declarer is missing an even number of cards in a suit he can expect them to split unevenly more often than not, while the likelihood with an odd number of missing cards is that they will split as evenly as possible. For example, a three-three break will occur only a little over one-third of the time, while a four-two break is a little over a 50% shot. Meanwhile, a straight finesse is an even-money bet, 50%. It would take some knowledge of the odds to get this first example right:

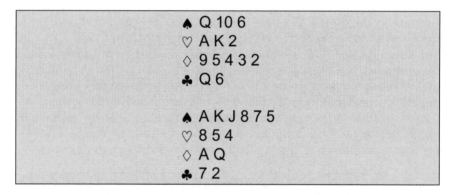

Against Four Spades, the defence began with two rounds of clubs followed by a switch to a low heart. The simple line is to take the diamond finesse and, if that fails, win the heart return, unblock the diamond, and hope to establish by ruffing and then cash a long diamond. This line will succeed when the diamond finesse wins, and also when the suit breaks three-three with trumps no worse than three-one, or four-two if trumps are two-two (necessary because of the shortage of entries to dummy). But both of those even splits are against the odds.

The best line, which will succeed whenever diamonds break either three-three or four-two, is to play ace and queen of the suit before drawing all the trumps. Declarer can win the heart return, ruff a diamond high, cross to the spade ten and ruff another diamond high if need be. Finally, draw trumps ending in dummy and cash the long diamond. There is just one more thing to consider, namely that a four-zero trump split would scupper this line as there would be no entry to the long diamond after trumps had been drawn, so cash one top trump in hand before playing off the diamond ace. If the trumps do happen to be four-zero, declarer will have to rely on the diamond finesse after all.

Sometimes, the best odds play will be easy to find.

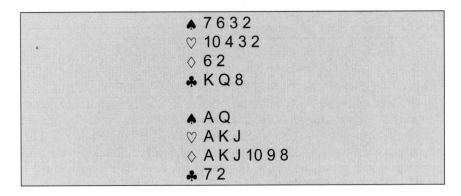

Declarer is in the contract of Five Diamonds on the lead of a club to the king and ace and a club back to the queen. In dummy for the one and only time, declarer would like to finesse in each of three suits. It must be correct to finesse in spades, however. If a red-suit finesse is taken, there is almost no chance of the spade king dropping under the ace, so there will always be a spade loser. In each of the red suits, it is true that the finesse is the best chance of avoiding a loser, but there is a realistic chance of the missing queen falling under the ace and king. In other words, by playing for the drop declarer has more chance of getting lucky in the red suits than in spades.

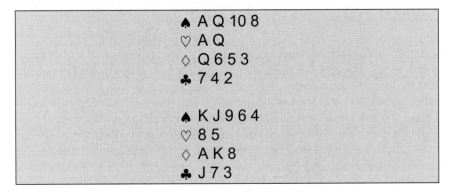

South plays Four Spades on the lead of the six of hearts. It is hard to read this intermediate card as being obviously from either strength or weakness, so the finesse appears to be a 50-50 proposition. Should declarer finesse at trick one, or should he win the ace, draw trumps and rely on an even diamond split?

It is correct to finesse. The finesse offers the aforementioned 50-50 chance, while a three-three diamond split will occur only a little over 35% of the time, much less likely.

# Combining Chances

Often, a combination of two chances may be better than relying on just one.

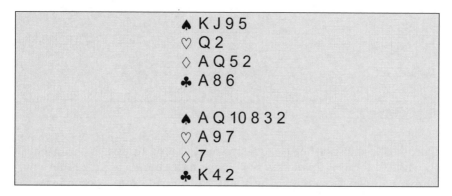

♠ K J 9 5
♡ Q 2
◇ A Q 5 2
♣ A 8 6

♠ A Q 10 8 3 2
♡ A 9 7
◇ 7
♣ K 4 2

In Six Spades, declarer receives the lead of the queen of clubs. After drawing trumps, he has a club loser and a heart loser. One possibility is to take the diamond finesse, which would permit a club discard on the ace of diamonds. The other hope is that the heart king might be with West, so that the lead of a low card towards the queen would produce a second heart trick and allow a club to be thrown from dummy on declarer's heart ace.

Each finesse is a 50% proposition, but it is important to start by taking the right one. If declarer takes a losing diamond finesse, he will not lose a club but he will still have to give up a heart for down one. However, if he first tries the play of a low heart towards the queen and that does not succeed, he gets the second chance of trying the diamond finesse to create a parking place for his club loser. By timing the play correctly, declarer gets to combine his chances, and the success of one finesse out of two is a 75% chance, meaning that the contract will fail only half as often as when just one chance is taken.

In this example, the key was to try the chance that involved giving up a trick even when it succeeded before the chance that might not involve giving up a trick.

The king of clubs is led against Seven Hearts. After drawing trumps, declarer can rely on a successful spade guess or on the ruffing diamond finesse. Which is the better play?

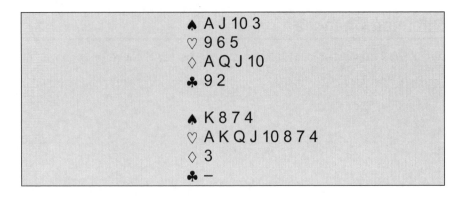

The answer is that neither is correct. The diamond finesse is a straight 50% shot, while a winning spade guess is marginally better because there may be a singleton queen. Looking at the spade suit in isolation, a second round finesse in one direction or the other is best, but in the context of the whole hand it is correct to cash the ace and king. That gives a significant possibility of dropping a doubleton queen, while if there is no luck in that suit, declarer can fall back on the ruffing diamond finesse, getting two chances instead of one.

## Points to Remember

♠ It helps to know how likely a play is to succeed. For example, that a choice between playing for a simple finesse or relying on a three-three break should be resolved in favour of the finesse because that has higher odds of success.

♠ Sometimes it may be possible to combine two or more chances rather than rely on only one possibility. Even though each of two possibilities offers less hope of success on its own than the one best chance, the combination of two chances may give a better overall hope of success.

♠ Generally, if one chance involves losing the lead even when it succeeds, it should be tried before a possibility that only loses a trick when it fails.

# Try it Yourself

In each case you are declarer, sitting South. How should you play to give yourself the best possible chance to make your contract?

### Question 1

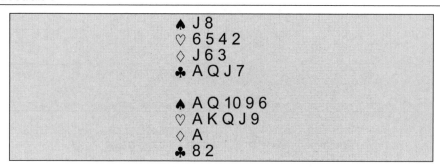

♠ J 8
♡ 6 5 4 2
♢ J 6 3
♣ A Q J 7

♠ A Q 10 9 6
♡ A K Q J 9
♢ A
♣ 8 2

| West | North | East | South |
|------|-------|------|-------|
|      |       |      | 2♣ |
| Pass | 2NT | Pass | 3♠ |
| Pass | 3NT | Pass | 4♡ |
| Pass | 5♣ (i) | Pass | 6♡ |
| All Pass |  |  |  |

(i) Cuebid

West leads the ten of diamonds.

### Question 2

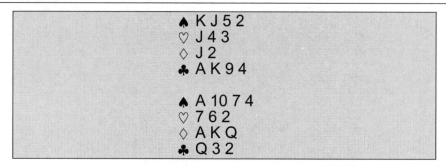

♠ K J 5 2
♡ J 4 3
♢ J 2
♣ A K 9 4

♠ A 10 7 4
♡ 7 6 2
♢ A K Q
♣ Q 3 2

| West | North | East | South |
|------|-------|------|-------|
|      |       |      | 1NT |
| Pass | 2♣ | Pass | 2♠ |
| Pass | 4♠ | All Pass |  |

West leads ace, king and a third heart to East's queen. East switches to the ten of diamonds. Play on.

## Question 3

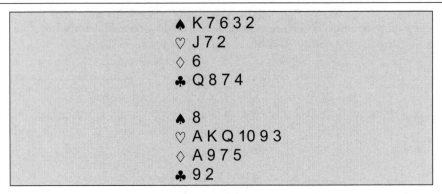

|  | ♠ K 7 6 3 2 |  |  |
|--|--|--|--|
|  | ♡ J 7 2 |  |  |
|  | ◊ 6 |  |  |
|  | ♣ Q 8 7 4 |  |  |
|  |  |  |  |
|  | ♠ 8 |  |  |
|  | ♡ A K Q 10 9 3 |  |  |
|  | ◊ A 9 7 5 |  |  |
|  | ♣ 9 2 |  |  |

| West | North | East | South |
|------|-------|------|-------|
|      |       |      | 1♡    |
| Dble | 2♡    | Pass | 4♡    |
| All Pass |    |      |       |

West leads the ace of clubs and switches to the four of hearts.

## Question 4

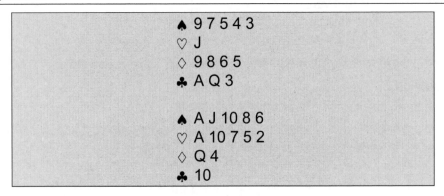

|  | ♠ 9 7 5 4 3 |  |  |
|--|--|--|--|
|  | ♡ J |  |  |
|  | ◊ 9 8 6 5 |  |  |
|  | ♣ A Q 3 |  |  |
|  |  |  |  |
|  | ♠ A J 10 8 6 |  |  |
|  | ♡ A 10 7 5 2 |  |  |
|  | ◊ Q 4 |  |  |
|  | ♣ 10 |  |  |

| West | North | East | South |
|------|-------|------|-------|
|      |       |      | 1♠    |
| Pass | 4♠    | All Pass |   |

The opening lead is the five of clubs.

## Question 5

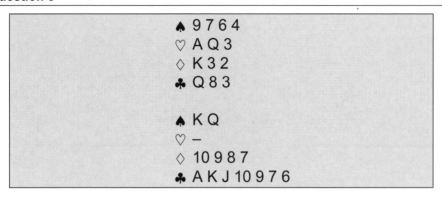

♠ 9 7 6 4
♡ A Q 3
◇ K 3 2
♣ Q 8 3

♠ K Q
♡ –
◇ 10 9 8 7
♣ A K J 10 9 7 6

| West | North | East | South |
|------|-------|------|-------|
|      |       |      | 5♣    |
| All Pass | | | |

The opening lead is the jack of hearts. When declarer puts in dummy's queen, it holds the trick.

## Question 6

♠ K 10 6 3
♡ 7
◇ A K J 9
♣ K 10 6 4

♠ A Q J 8 4
♡ Q 8 5
◇ 10 6
♣ A J 2

| West | North | East | South |
|------|-------|------|-------|
|      |       |      | 1♠    |
| Pass | 2♣    | Pass | 2♠    |
| Pass | 3♡    | Pass | 3NT   |
| Pass | 5♠    | Pass | 6♠    |
| All Pass | | | |

West leads the ace then six of hearts.

## Question 7

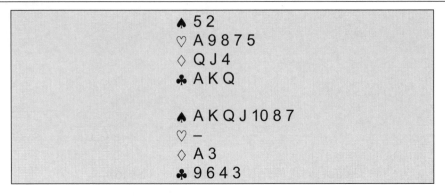

♠ K 8 6
♡ A 8 5 4
◇ Q J 2
♣ 10 9 2

♠ A Q 10 9 5 4
♡ Q 6 3
◇ A K
♣ A Q

| West | North | East | South |
|------|-------|------|-------|
|      |       |      | 2♣    |
| Pass | 2NT   | Pass | 3♠    |
| Pass | 4♡ (i)| Pass | 6♠    |
| All Pass |    |      |       |

(i) Cuebid

West leads the jack of spades, East playing the two.

## Question 8

♠ 5 2
♡ A 9 8 7 5
◇ Q J 4
♣ A K Q

♠ A K Q J 10 8 7
♡ –
◇ A 3
♣ 9 6 4 3

| West | North | East | South |
|------|-------|------|-------|
|      |       |      | 2♠    |
| Pass | 4NT   | Pass | 5♡    |
| Pass | 5NT   | Pass | 7♠    |
| All Pass |    |      |       |

The opening lead is the queen of hearts.

## Question 9

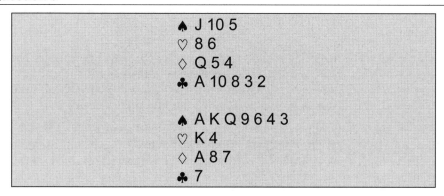

♠ J 10 5
♡ 8 6
◊ Q 5 4
♣ A 10 8 3 2

♠ A K Q 9 6 4 3
♡ K 4
◊ A 8 7
♣ 7

| West | North | East | South |
|------|-------|------|-------|
|      |       |      | 2♠ |
| Pass | 2NT | Pass | 3♠ |
| Pass | 4♠ | All Pass | |

West leads the king of clubs.

## Question 10

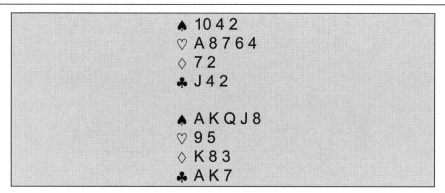

♠ 10 4 2
♡ A 8 7 6 4
◊ 7 2
♣ J 4 2

♠ A K Q J 8
♡ 9 5
◊ K 8 3
♣ A K 7

| West | North | East | South |
|------|-------|------|-------|
|      |       |      | 1♠ |
| Pass | 2♠ | Pass | 4♠ |
| All Pass | | | |

West leads the king of hearts.

# Solutions

## Question 1

Declarer wins the ace of diamonds and draws trumps in three rounds. Many players would see this as a matter of trying two finesses and succeeding if one or both kings proved to be onside. However, a little flexibility of mind will show that it is actually correct to not take any finesse at all.

Declarer can simply play ace and another spade and assure himself of four winners in that suit. That enables him to throw three clubs from the dummy, and the twelfth trick is made by ruffing the club loser with dummy's last trump.

## Question 2

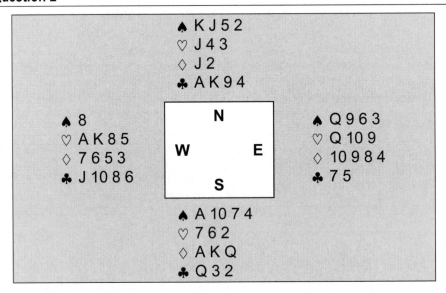

The message of this deal is to cherish your spot cards. It looks like a straight two-way finesse for the missing trump queen. However, while it really is a guess should the trumps be splitting three-two, there is a small extra chance to take advantage of if they are four-one.

If there is a singleton eight or nine of trumps, there will always be a loser if it is West who holds the length – try it and see. But if East holds the length it can be picked up without loss. Start with the king of spades, seeing the eight or nine fall from West. Continue with the jack to the queen and ace. The ten, seven are sitting over the nine, six, and declarer crosses to dummy and takes a second spade finesse.

A small extra chance, perhaps, but it costs nothing to play for it in what would otherwise be an out-and-out guess situation.

## Question 3

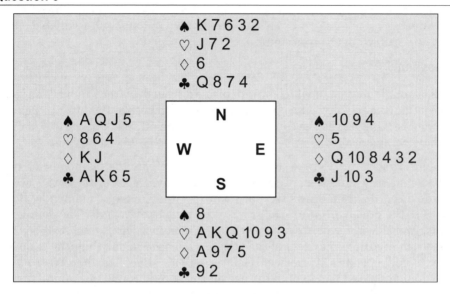

```
              ♠ K 7 6 3 2
              ♡ J 7 2
              ◇ 6
              ♣ Q 8 7 4

♠ A Q J 5        N          ♠ 10 9 4
♡ 8 6 4                     ♡ 5
◇ K J        W     E        ◇ Q 10 8 4 3 2
♣ A K 6 5                   ♣ J 10 3
                 S
              ♠ 8
              ♡ A K Q 10 9 3
              ◇ A 9 7 5
              ♣ 9 2
```

It would be nice to be able to take two diamond ruffs in the dummy, but it looks as though this may not be possible. The problem is that if declarer takes a diamond ruff immediately, he has no quick entry back to hand to take a second ruff, and as soon as the defenders gain the lead they will surely lead a second round of trumps to prevent that second ruff.

Either the spade king or club queen can be established, perhaps even both, though this may mean not even getting one diamond ruff. Nonetheless, it must be correct to play to establish these high cards. At trick three, declarer plays a spade towards the king. West wins and plays a second trump, East discarding a diamond. Again, one diamond ruff is no use. There is one slim chance remaining. West is marked with the king of clubs. If declarer leads up to the queen West will have to take the king. Of course, he will return his last trump, preventing even one ruff in dummy. But if East holds precisely ♣ J10x, the eight of clubs will be declarer's tenth trick. Again, a slim chance, but the best there is.

## Question 4

There are three losers and it may be tempting to take the club finesse to dispose of a diamond from hand. However, a losing finesse would guarantee one down on East's likely diamond switch. Better is to win the club ace. With so many hearts to ruff, declarer cannot afford to play safe in the trump suit by taking a first-round finesse. He may be tempted to cash the ace of trumps therefore then set about the hearts. That will be good enough if hearts split four-three, but on a five-two break declarer will be short of an entry to take the last heart ruff.

The best play is to win the ace of clubs and immediately play ace of hearts, then ruff a heart. Now play a spade to the ace and take a second heart ruff. The delayed spade play provides an extra entry to hand, after which declarer can crossruff to his heart's content.

## Question 5

It is a simple matter of which suit to discard from declarer's hand. The temptation may be to throw two clubs, retaining the power of the king and queen of spades. This leaves the contract reliant on the 50% shot of the ace of diamonds being onside.

The alternative is to throw the spades and try to play the diamonds for two tricks and only two losers. That is the better play. Declarer takes the two spade discards, then draws trumps. Now he runs the ten of diamonds. If that loses to the queen or jack he later runs the nine of diamonds. The double finesse works whenever West has either the queen or jack, which will be the case roughly three-quarters of the time, as opposed to only half the time for him to hold specifically the ace. Declarer will also succeed when West holds ace doubleton and has to play the ace on the second round, assuming trumps to be two-one so that the fourth diamond can be ruffed in dummy.

If trumps are three-zero declarer will require diamonds to be three-three or West to hold a doubleton queen or jack.

## Question 6

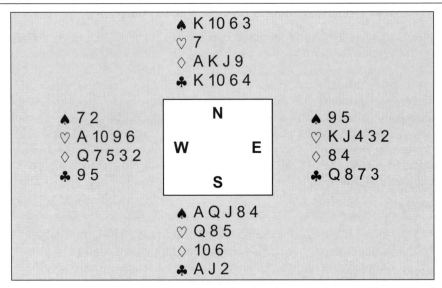

Declarer ruffs the second heart and draws trumps, ruffing his last heart along the way. The twelfth trick may come from a finesse in either direction in either minor. Better is the possibility to cash the ace and king of one suit to see if the queen falls, and only if that hope does not materialise fall back on a guess in the other suit.

Which ace, king should be cashed? Holding seven clubs to only six diamonds, it might appear that there is more likely to be a doubleton queen of clubs out than a doubleton queen of diamonds. Quite true. However, the advantage of cashing the diamonds is that a third round can be ruffed, catering to the chance of either defender holding queen to three diamonds as well as queen doubleton.

That is the correct way to combine the chances in the two suits – play three rounds of diamonds, ruffing the third one. Even if nothing good happens, it may be that declarer will see enough to be able to form an opinion as to which defender is more likely to have the length in clubs, making the guess in that suit a better than even-money proposition. In the diagram position, the five-two diamond break provides the clue to play East for the club queen.

### Question 7

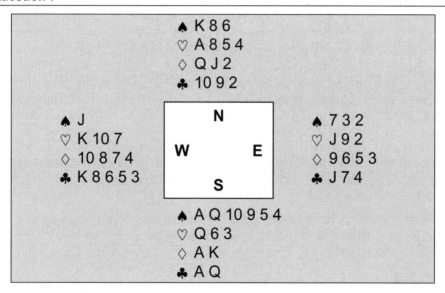

There are eleven top tricks and it is easy to see two chances for getting one more – East could hold either the heart or club king. It must be correct to try for the heart to be onside before the club. A losing club finesse means that it is too late to try the heart, as even when the heart is onside declarer has two losers. If declarer draws trumps then plays a heart towards the queen, he has the two chances mentioned above, but there is a third possibility, namely a three-three heart split. This is the way to play it to combine all three possibilities:

Win the opening lead in dummy and play a low heart immediately. Say that the queen loses to the king and West returns a diamond. Declarer can win, unblock the second diamond and cross to the ace of hearts. Next he throws his last heart on the queen of diamonds and ruffs a heart high. If the hearts break three-three, declarer draws trumps ending in dummy and cashes the long heart. If not, he again draws trumps ending in dummy but this time has to fall back on the club finesse, having tried all three of his chances in turn.

## Question 8

Again declarer has three chances for his contract and must find the best line of play to combine them. The chances are an even heart break, the jack and ten of clubs falling in three rounds, and the diamond finesse. If declarer wins the heart ace at trick one he has to discard something from hand and now either the club or diamond chance is wasted.

So declarer ruffs the opening lead and draws trumps, throwing a diamond from dummy if a third round is required. Now he crosses to a top club and ruffs a heart, crosses back to a second top club and ruffs a third heart. Finally, he crosses to the last club honour and cashes the ace of hearts. If the hearts are four-three he has two heart tricks and thirteen in all. If hearts are five-two, by now he knows whether the nine of clubs is a winner or not. If not, he discards it and relies on the diamond finesse.

## Question 9

This is a pretty good contract. It will succeed if either the heart king or diamond queen is a winner, plus there is the possibility of both black suits dividing evenly. Declarer wins the club lead and ruffs a club high, preserving his small trumps to cross to dummy later in the play. A spade to the jack allows a second high club ruff. If both black suits have divided as wished, a spade to the ten will permit a third club ruff and a spade to the five will now allow the fifth club to be cashed.

If either black suit has broken badly, declarer draws trumps ending in dummy and leads a heart to the king. His last chance will be to try a diamond to the queen.

## Question 10

Declarer's main chance is that the ace of diamonds will be onside, when he will be able to make his king then take a diamond ruff for the tenth trick. There is a secondary though poor chance that the club queen will fall doubleton. Is there any other possibility?

The hearts may split three-three. Declarer should duck the opening lead. On anything but a trump switch, declarer can play to ruff the third round of hearts and, if they divide evenly, draw trumps ending in dummy. If the hearts prove to be four-two, declarer crosses to the ten of spades and leads a diamond up, hoping for the king to be a winner and to get a subsequent ruff.

If West switches to a trump at trick two it will not be possible to combine the chances in the red suits. If declarer tests the hearts first, he will be in the wrong hand to play a diamond towards the king, so will have to cross to the spade ten to do so should hearts not behave as he desires. Now the defence will be able to play a third trump when they take their diamond trick, and there will be no ruff in the dummy. On a spade switch, declarer should just win in dummy and play a diamond up, giving up on the possibility of an even break in both majors.

# Chapter Six

# Card Reading

♡   **Clues from the Auction**

♡   **Clues from the Opening Lead**

♡   **Points to Remember**

♡   **Try it Yourself**

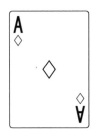

# Clues from the Auction

The auction can often provide valuable clues as to the position of missing high cards. So too can the line of defence chosen by your opponents. When you use these clues to help to decide your best approach to the play of a hand, you are using a technique called Card Reading.

Unless the opposition is very weak, it is reasonable to base your line of play on the assumption that an opponent who does not make a particular bid or play cannot have a suitable hand for that particular bid or play. It is easy to take note of the things that actually happen but, just as in the famous Sherlock Holmes tale of the dog that did not bark in the night, so at the bridge table it is often the things that do not happen that are the most revealing. Here are a few of the many reliable inferences from the auction:

(i) A player who has an opportunity to open the bidding and does not take it will have less than a good 12 HCP.

(ii) A player who opens with one of a suit will not have both a balanced hand and be within his agreed range for a One No-trump opening bid.

(iii) A player who passes his partner's one of a suit opening, playing standard methods, will have less than 6 HCP.

(iv) A player who does not overcall at the one level will not hold both a good five-card suit and an outside ace or king.

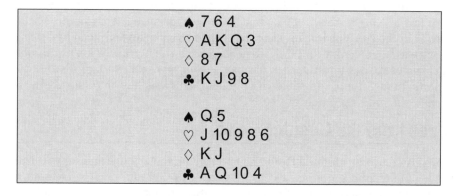

♠ 7 6 4
♡ A K Q 3
◇ 8 7
♣ K J 9 8

♠ Q 5
♡ J 10 9 8 6
◇ K J
♣ A Q 10 4

South opens One Heart and plays in Four Hearts after an uncontested auction. West leads the jack of spades to East's ace, and back comes the spade eight to the queen and king. West plays the ten of spades next, East following with the three. Declarer ruffs and draws trumps, after which it is all down to his view of the diamond situation.

The defensive carding suggests that East started with ace to three spades, it being normal to return the original fourth highest at trick two but the top of the two remaining if starting with three cards. In that case West must have begun with king, jack, ten to five spades. Had he also held the ace of diamonds, he would surely have overcalled One Spade. Accordingly, declarer should play a diamond to the king, playing East to hold the ace.

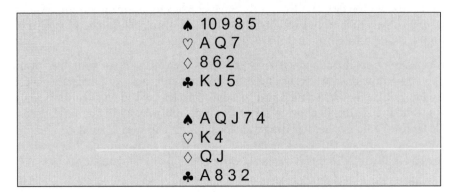

South opens One Spade after three passes and plays in Four Spades with no opposition bidding. West leads ace, king and a third diamond, declarer ruffing. South crosses to dummy with the king of hearts to take the spade finesse but there is no joy there as West wins the king and exits with the jack of hearts.

After winning the heart switch and drawing trumps, declarer can take one club pitch on the queen of hearts, but still has three clubs in each hand and cannot afford another loser. He cannot be sure of success, indeed, more often than not he may go down, but what he knows for sure is that he must not take the club finesse, but must instead cash the ace and king. Why? Because West passed as dealer and has turned up with the ace and king of diamonds, the king of spades and the jack of hearts. That gives him 11 HCP, and there is no room for him to also hold the queen of clubs as he would surely have opened the bidding if holding 13 HCP.

# Clues from the Opening Lead

More clues can be gleaned from the opening lead. Most defenders will find the lead of a solid sequence a very attractive option, as such leads combine safety with the possibility of cashing or establishing tricks fairly quickly. It follows that a player who leads a low card probably has no such sequence. This next example illustrates this:

*(see following diagram)*

West opens One Club and North and East both pass. After South overcalls Two Spades, intermediate, he plays in Four Spades. West leads the three of diamonds. There are three club losers and a spade finesse into the hand that opened the bidding. It may seem that a diamond finesse at trick one, allowing a losing club to be thrown on the diamond ace, is more likely to succeed than the spade finesse. Card reading confirms this idea. If West had been looking at both the ace and king of clubs he would almost certainly have led one of them rather than make a dangerous lead in another suit. So East must hold one of those two cards. Once we give East at least the king of clubs, there is no room for him to hold another king. It is not so much that West opened the bidding, as he might well do so with 11 HCP if he has a little distribution to improve his hand; rather, it is the fact that East passed over his partner's One Club opening. Had he held two kings, it would have been normal for him to find a response.

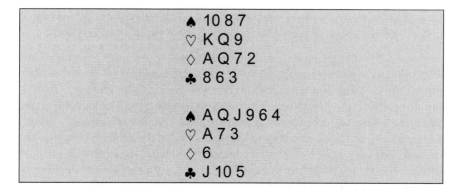

So the combination of the auction and opening lead tells declarer that he can finesse at trick one in almost perfect safety. After the diamond queen has won the first trick, declarer cashes the ace to pitch a club loser, then plays a spade to the ace – there is no point in taking a finesse known to be wrong. Once in a while, when the spade king is bare, declarer even makes an overtrick.

This next contract was quite a poor one, as there was a danger of a diamond ruff, quite apart from the missing trump queen to worry about.

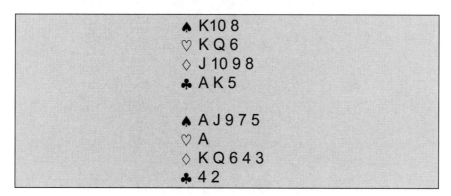

| West | North | East | South |
|------|-------|------|-------|
| – | – | – | 1♠ |
| Pass | 2◇ | Pass | 4◇ |
| Pass | 4NT | Pass | 5♡ |
| Pass | 6♠ | All Pass | |

West led the ace followed by the seven of diamonds, East following both times, much to declarer's relief. It seemed strange to declarer that West had attacked his main side suit, in which he might well have had a critical decision to make. There was little prospect that West, who held only a doubleton diamond, would be giving his partner a ruff, so why lead diamonds?

There was only one answer that made any sense at all, namely that West wanted to make 100% certain of making his diamond ace – though where he thought it was going to run to only he knew – because he thought that he had a likely second trick elsewhere. That had to be the queen of spades, so declarer took a first round finesse by running the nine of spades and, when that won, continued with a second spade to dummy's ten. When West showed up with queen to four spades, declarer was very pleased indeed with his card-reading. The panicky opening lead of the ace of diamonds gave declarer the clue he needed to make his slam.

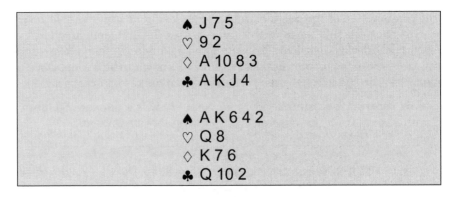

♠ J 7 5
♡ 9 2
◇ A 10 8 3
♣ A K J 4

♠ A K 6 4 2
♡ Q 8
◇ K 7 6
♣ Q 10 2

| West | North | East | South |
|------|-------|------|-------|
| – | 1◇ | Dble | Rdbl |
| 1♡ | Pass | Pass | 1♠ |
| Pass | 2♠ | Pass | 4♠ |
| All Pass | | | |

West leads the five of hearts to East's king. East cashes the ace of hearts, West dropping the three, and switches to the queen of diamonds.

Declarer has no need to worry about a diamond loser as his third diamond can eventually be discarded on dummy's fourth club. No, his only worry is the trump suit. Most declarers, with no clues to suggest an alternative, would play off the ace and king of spades, succeeding whenever the suit broke three-two or there was a bare queen. However, there is a much stronger line, suggested by East's take-out double.

It is just possible that West holds the queen of spades but rather unlikely. The double suggests that East should have the length in spades along with the queen. If the suit is three-two then any sensible line of play should succeed, but what if East holds four cards?

Declarer should win the diamond switch in dummy and lead the jack of spades. That will go to the queen and ace. If East began with ♠ Q1098, nothing can be done, but if West has the bare ten, nine or eight, it will be pinned on the first round. Declarer continues by leading low to the seven and East wins with, say, the nine. Whether East plays a club or a diamond next, declarer wins in dummy, while on a heart lead he ruffs in hand and crosses to the ace of clubs. He can now lead the five of spades for a finesse of the seven then cash the top trump and claim his contract.

## Points to Remember

♠ The auction offers many clues to help declarer to find the winning line of play. Not only the bids that are made by the eventual defenders, but also those bids they did not make, help to give a picture of their holdings.

♠ The opening lead also offers clues about that defender's holding. For example, most defenders will favour a solid sequence lead rather than a dangerous lead of a low card from a broken honour holding, so the lead of a low card tends to deny holding a sequence elsewhere in the hand.

♠ If the clues from bidding and defence tell you that the normal play in a suit cannot succeed, do not be afraid to play against the odds to give yourself a chance for success.

# Try it Yourself

In each case you are declarer, sitting South. How should you play to give yourself the best possible chance to make your contract?

### Question 1

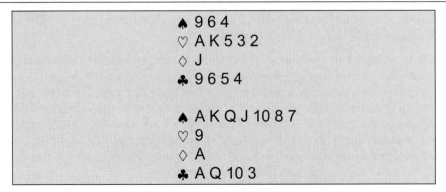

♠ 9 6 4
♡ A K 5 3 2
♢ J
♣ 9 6 5 4

♠ A K Q J 10 8 7
♡ 9
♢ A
♣ A Q 10 3

| West | North | East | South |
|------|-------|------|-------|
|      |       |      | 2♣    |
| 3♡   | Dble  | Pass | 4♠    |
| Pass | 5♡    | Pass | 6♠    |
| All Pass |   |      |       |

West leads the queen of hearts.

### Question 2

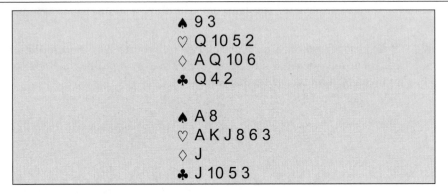

♠ 9 3
♡ Q 10 5 2
♢ A Q 10 6
♣ Q 4 2

♠ A 8
♡ A K J 8 6 3
♢ J
♣ J 10 5 3

| West | North | East | South |
|------|-------|------|-------|
| Pass | Pass  | Pass | 1♡    |
| 1♠   | 3♡    | 4♠   | 5♡    |
| All Pass |   |      |       |

The opening lead is the five of spades to East's king.

## Question 3

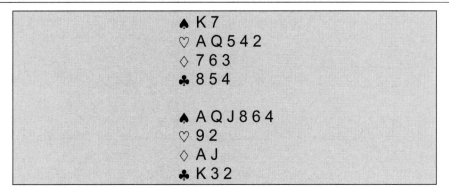

♠ K 7
♡ A Q 5 4 2
◇ 7 6 3
♣ 8 5 4

♠ A Q J 8 6 4
♡ 9 2
◇ A J
♣ K 3 2

| West | North | East | South |
|------|-------|------|-------|
|      |       | 1◇   | 1♠    |
| Pass | 2♡    | Pass | 3♠    |
| Pass | 4♠    | All Pass |   |

West leads the king of diamonds.

## Question 4

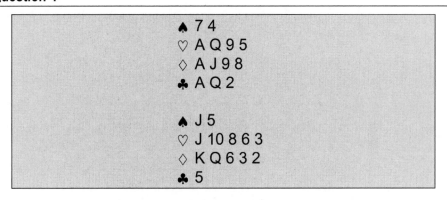

♠ 7 4
♡ A Q 9 5
◇ A J 9 8
♣ A Q 2

♠ J 5
♡ J 10 8 6 3
◇ K Q 6 3 2
♣ 5

| West | North | East | South |
|------|-------|------|-------|
|      |       | 1♠   | Pass  |
| 2♠   | Dble  | Pass | 4♡    |
| All Pass |   |      |       |

West leads the three of spades to East's ace. East switches to the seven of diamonds.

## Question 5

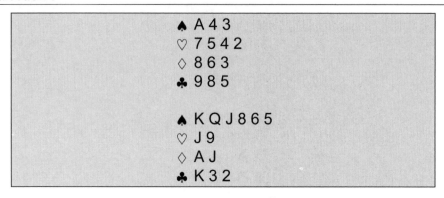

♠ A 4 3
♡ 7 5 4 2
◇ 8 6 3
♣ 9 8 5

♠ K Q J 8 6 5
♡ J 9
◇ A J
♣ K 3 2

| West | North | East | South |
|------|-------|------|-------|
| 1♡ | Pass | 1NT | 2♠ |
| All Pass | | | |

The opening lead is the four of diamonds to East's king.

## Question 6

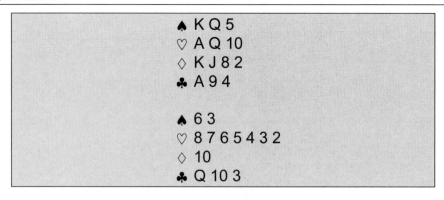

♠ K Q 5
♡ A Q 10
◇ K J 8 2
♣ A 9 4

♠ 6 3
♡ 8 7 6 5 4 3 2
◇ 10
♣ Q 10 3

| West | North | East | South |
|------|-------|------|-------|
| 1NT(i) | Dble | 2◇ | 2♡ |
| Pass | 4♡ | All Pass | |

(i) 15-17

West leads the jack of spades to king and ace. Back comes a second spade.

**Question 7**

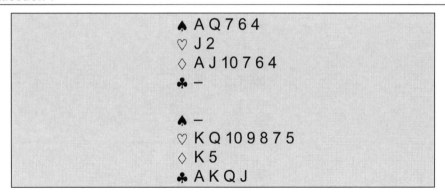

♠ A Q 7 6 4
♡ J 2
◇ A J 10 7 6 4
♣ —

♠ —
♡ K Q 10 9 8 7 5
◇ K 5
♣ A K Q J

| West | North | East | South |
|------|-------|------|-------|
|      |       |      | 2♡    |
| Pass | 3◇    | Pass | 3♡    |
| Pass | 3♠    | Pass | 3NT   |
| Pass | 6♡    | All Pass |    |

West leads the two of diamonds.

**Question 8**

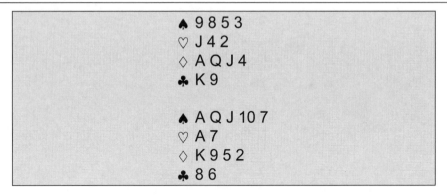

♠ 9 8 5 3
♡ J 4 2
◇ A Q J 4
♣ K 9

♠ A Q J 10 7
♡ A 7
◇ K 9 5 2
♣ 8 6

| West | North | East | South |
|------|-------|------|-------|
| Pass | Pass  | Pass | 1♠    |
| Pass | 3♠    | Pass | 4♠    |
| All Pass |   |      |       |

West leads the nine of hearts, East following with the six.

## Question 9

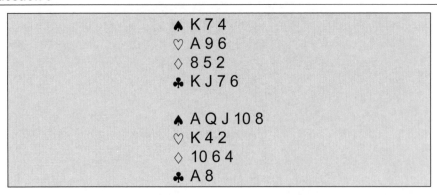

♠ K 7 4
♡ A 9 6
♢ 8 5 2
♣ K J 7 6

♠ A Q J 10 8
♡ K 4 2
♢ 10 6 4
♣ A 8

| West | North | East | South |
|------|-------|------|-------|
| Pass | Pass | Pass | 1♠ |
| 2♡ | 3♠ | Pass | 4♠ |
| All Pass | | | |

West leads the ace of diamonds followed by the diamond king and queen. He switches to the jack of hearts. Play on.

## Question 10

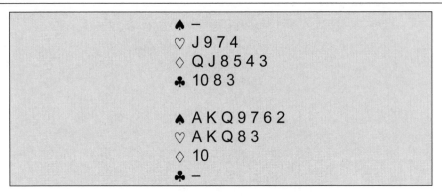

♠ —
♡ J 9 7 4
♢ Q J 8 5 4 3
♣ 10 8 3

♠ A K Q 9 7 6 2
♡ A K Q 8 3
♢ 10
♣ —

| West | North | East | South |
|------|-------|------|-------|
| | | | 2♣ |
| Dble | Pass | 5♣ | 5♠ |
| Dble | Pass | Pass | 6♡ |
| Pass | Pass | Dble | All Pass |

The opening lead is the king of clubs.

# Solutions

## Question 1

It appears that declarer must merely hold his club losers to one, until he considers the bidding. That Three Heart overcall is likely to be based on a seven-card suit, meaning that the opening lead is about to be ruffed, after which declarer will not be able to afford a club loser. With only the nine of spades in dummy as an entry to take club finesses, this will be a tall order.

In fact, things are not quite as bleak as at first sight, but declarer will have to show a little imagination. He should duck the opening lead and play low again if West leads a second heart, ruffing in hand. After winning trick two declarer draws trumps ending in dummy. Two clubs can go away on the carefully preserved ace and king of hearts, after which a club to the queen will decide the fate of the contract.

## Question 2

There are three losers but there is a two-way diamond finesse that could provide a parking place for the spade loser. But who has the diamond king?

The combination of bidding and opening lead has been very revealing. West has a queen-high spade suit, probably also missing the jack as he would usually lead queen from queen, jack. He is unlikely to hold both the top clubs as then he would have led one of them. That makes him heavy favourite to hold the diamond king for his overcall. Declarer should draw a couple of rounds of trumps, then run the jack of diamonds. If there is still a trump out he draws it in the process of crossing to dummy to cash the ace of diamonds, after which it is a simple matter to concede two club tricks.

## Question 3

There is a diamond to lose plus two clubs – the club ace will surely be onside after East's opening bid. What about the king of hearts? Well, unfortunately that is almost certainly offside as otherwise East has opened with at most 10 HCP. It appears that there are four losers then. There is one chance, to find East with only a singleton or doubleton heart, when the heart queen can be made into a winner.

Declarer wins the opening lead and draws trumps, then leads a heart and ducks it completely. Say that East wins and cashes the queen of diamonds, then switches to the queen of clubs. As East is marked with the club ace, declarer puts up the king, then cashes his trumps. Finally, he leads a heart to the ace and, with any luck, the king falls, leaving the queen as declarer's tenth trick.

## Question 4

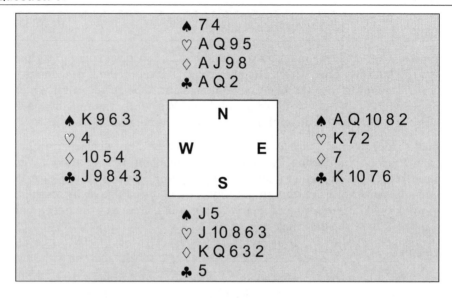

| West | North | East | South |
|------|-------|------|-------|
| | | 1♠ | Pass |
| 2♠ | Dble | Pass | 4♡ |
| All Pass | | | |

West leads the three of spades to East's ace. East switches to the seven of diamonds.

If the ace of spades is a true card, West holds the king and East will hold the king of hearts to make up his opening bid. That would not be fatal in itself, but that diamond switch screams of a singleton and it appears that East thinks he is going to win the heart king and cross to his partner's spade king to get a diamond ruff. Is there any way to avoid this?

East's play suggests that he holds three hearts, as otherwise declarer could just play ace and another trump to prevent the ruff. We have not considered the club position, however, and that is the key to declarer's success, unlikely though this may seem.

Declarer cannot afford to concede a trick to the king of hearts while West has an entry, so he must be deprived of that entry. Declarer should win the diamond switch and cash the heart ace. Then he plays the ace of clubs and queen of clubs and, when East covers with the king, discards his spade loser. This Scissors Coup means that East can no longer reach his partner's hand to get his ruff and brings home the contract. And if East does not cover the club? He can see what you are trying to do and is testing your nerve. Discard the spade anyway as this is easily the best chance of success.

## Question 5

This would appear to be a very simple hand. To make Two Spades, declarer must make a trick with the king of clubs. The opening lead is rather ominous, however. East has turned up with the king of diamonds and will surely also hold a heart honour, most likely the king, as West would have preferred to lead from two touching heart honours rather than from queen to some number of diamonds.

If East has the two red kings he will not also hold the club ace on this auction. Declarer should win the first trick and draw trumps, then play a low club from both hands. When he regains the lead, he ducks another club and crosses his fingers. If West has only ace doubleton club the ace will appear, and the king will be declarer's eighth trick.

## Question 6

Declarer can see 21 HCP between his hand and dummy and East has just played an ace. West should have every other high card for his One No-trump opening bid.

Declarer wins the second spade in dummy, then ruffs the third spade. He should lead a heart to the ten with some confidence, then lead a diamond off the table. West will win but can do nothing to cause a problem. When declarer regains the lead he ruffs a diamond to get to hand then takes another heart finesse and cashes the ace of hearts. Knowing where the missing honours are lying, it is a simple matter to force a second club trick (he can also ruff out the ace of diamonds to establish a winner).

## Question 7

This one looks so easy that a careless declarer might go down without giving the matter any thought. The opening lead may be from queen to four but is more likely to be a singleton. Either way, if declarer wins the first trick and plays a trump there is a big risk of an adverse ruff if the heart ace is in the same hand as the diamond length. The solution is simple. Declarer should win the ace of diamonds and cash the ace of spades, on which he throws the king of diamonds. Now he can play on trumps with no danger of conceding a fatal ruff.

## Question 8

With one heart loser, declarer will succeed if either the ace of clubs is onside or he can avoid a trump loser. It looks simple enough – cross to dummy with a diamond and take the spade finesse. If that loses, there is still the chance that the club ace will be onside.

The diamond play is actually a little dangerous because it might establish a diamond ruff for East should West hold the spade king. This is one of those slightly unusual hands on which, if the spade finesse is working, there is no need to take it. Why?

The opening lead seems to mark East with the king and queen of hearts. If he also holds the king of spades he cannot have the ace of clubs, as he would then surely have opened the bidding. So whenever the spade finesse is working so is the club finesse. The dangerous layout is the one in which West holds the spade king and East the club ace. In that case the only hope is that the spade king is bare.

Correct play is to win the opening lead and lay down the ace of spades. If the king drops all well and good. Whether or not it does so, declarer continues to draw trumps. Later he leads to the king of clubs. If East did turn up with the spade king, he can do so with some confidence. If the spade was with West there are no guarantees about the club, but at least declarer knows that he has given it his best shot.

## Question 9

West passed as dealer yet has already shown up with 10 HCP. He is then very unlikely to hold the queen of clubs. This is bad news for declarer, as the best chance of finding a parking place for his third heart would otherwise have been the club finesse. Perhaps the club can be ruffed out by playing three rounds?

Declarer wins the heart in hand to preserve a late entry to a possible third club trick. He draws three rounds of trumps ending in dummy, and discovers that West held three trumps. Is there any hope?

West has shown up with five hearts for his overcall and three cards in each of diamonds and spades, so can have at most two clubs. What declarer must hope for is that West holds either the ten or nine of clubs. Having drawn trumps, he leads the club jack off the table, which East must cover. Now a second club goes to the king. If West had a singleton or doubleton ten or nine, dummy's seven, six of clubs are now equals against East's nine or ten, and the ruffing finesse creates the tenth trick for declarer.

As I may have said before, cherish your spot cards.

## Question 10

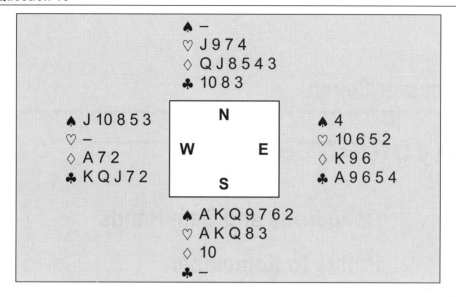

| West | North | East | South |
|------|-------|------|-------|
|      |       |      | 2♣ |
| Dble | Pass | 5♣ | 5♠ |
| Dble | Pass | Pass | 6♡ |
| Pass | Pass | Dble | All Pass |

The opening lead is the king of clubs.

There is only one reason why West could have doubled Five Spades – he must have length in spades. If the suit is breaking six-zero there is no hope, but a five-one split need not be fatal as declarer can take one low ruff and one high ruff in dummy. However, it is not quite so straightforward because declarer has just been forced at trick one and East's final double suggests that the trumps may also break badly. What if they are four-zero?

Declarer cannot afford to ruff again in hand so his communications must be within the trump suit, which means that he must show a little care. Having ruffed the opening lead declarer ruffs a low spade, taking care to use dummy's nine. Now he leads a low heart to the ace, confirming the four-zero break. That is no longer a problem. Declarer ruffs a second spade with the jack of hearts then leads the remaining low trump to his eight, draws trumps and cashes the spades.

# Chapter Seven

# Avoidance Play

♡ **Dangerous and Safe Hands**

♡ **Points to Remember**

♡ **Try it Yourself**

 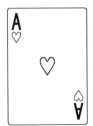 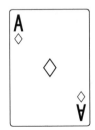 

# Dangerous and Safe Hands

There are standard ways in which to play many suit combinations but, while it is good to know these, a little learning can be a dangerous thing. Suits should not always be looked at in isolation; rather, declarer should consider his play in relation to the whole hand.

Often, declarer may have a weak spot, but one which is vulnerable to attack by only one defender and not the other. Clearly, if we have to lose the lead we would prefer to do so to the Safe hand, the defender who cannot attack our weak spot, rather than the Dangerous hand. This leads to the idea of the Avoidance Play, keeping the Dangerous opponent off lead.

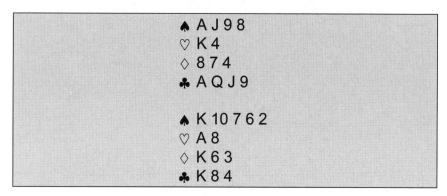

The contract is Four Spades on the lead of the queen of hearts. In isolation, the percentage play missing queen to four of a suit is to cash the ace and king, but is that correct here? Declarer can afford to lose a trick to the queen of trumps as there are still ten tricks – four spades, four clubs and two hearts, but only if it is West who wins the trick, as he cannot attack the diamond weak spot effectively. Correct play is to win the heart lead and play ace of spades, then run the jack. This avoids the risk of East gaining the lead to push a diamond honour through the king.

```
            ♠ K 8 4
            ♡ K 10 6
            ◇ A Q 10 9 6
            ♣ 10 4

            ♠ 7 5
            ♡ A J 9 8 6
            ◇ K J
            ♣ A J 3 2
```

## Suit Contracts

This example is a little more complex but the same basic principle applies. Against Four Hearts, West leads a low club to East's king. Declarer has ten tricks even if he loses to the queen of trumps, but a lead through the king of spades could be dangerous. He can ensure that West does not gain the lead with the trump queen by taking a first round finesse, running the nine and, if that holds, continuing with a low card to the ten. But this time a little more work is required. If declarer wins the opening lead and takes the recommended line in the trump suit, East may win the queen and put his partner in with the club queen to lead a spade through. The solution is simple; duck the opening lead, win the continuation then play as suggested. Now West can have no entry so cannot threaten the contract.

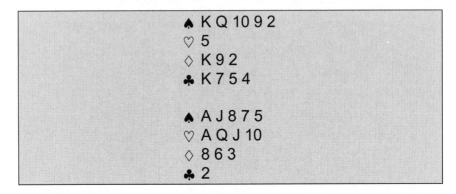

Once again the contract is Four Spades, the opening lead being the queen of clubs. The danger is that the ace of diamonds may be over the king, giving four losers. However, the heart suit offers the possibility of establishing sufficient winners to take care of the diamond position.

After drawing trumps, a simple heart finesse would create a second trick and allow one discard, but if the finesse lost West might be able to switch to a diamond through the king. The alternative is the ruffing heart finesse, winning the ace then leading the queen, discarding a diamond from dummy if the king is not played. Even if East wins the heart king, he can cash only one diamond trick, so cannot hurt us. And if East does not take the ace of diamonds he will lose it, as the remaining diamonds can be pitched on the jack and ten of hearts. One important point; declarer must cover the queen of clubs at trick one, even though he expects the ace to be over the king. If he does not, West, the danger hand, will retain the lead and may find the killing diamond switch.

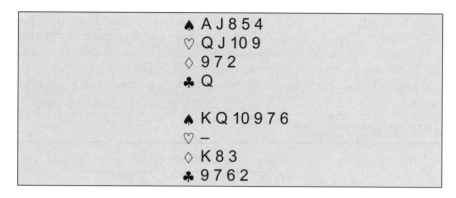

♠ A J 8 5 4
♡ Q J 10 9
◇ 9 7 2
♣ Q

♠ K Q 10 9 7 6
♡ –
◇ K 8 3
♣ 9 7 6 2

West leads the ace and king of clubs against Four Spades. Declarer ruffs the second club in dummy. The simple play is to rely on East to hold the ace of diamonds, a straight 50% chance. There is something much better, however. Take the double ruffing finesse in hearts, leading the queen and discarding a diamond from hand. If this loses, West cannot lead diamonds to good effect so may exit with a third club. That is ruffed in dummy and trumps drawn. Now the jack of hearts is led and again declarer pitches a diamond if an honour does not appear. The double finesse will succeed when East holds either or both of the missing heart honours, a roughly 75% chance.

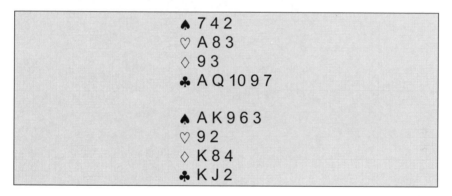

♠ 7 4 2
♡ A 8 3
◇ 9 3
♣ A Q 10 9 7

♠ A K 9 6 3
♡ 9 2
◇ K 8 4
♣ K J 2

West leads the king of hearts against our contract of Four Spades. If trumps divide evenly we can see ten tricks: four trumps, five clubs and the ace of hearts. The danger is that we may lose four: a trump, a heart and two diamonds. There will be two diamond losers only if East can get the lead to attack from the dangerous hand, so this is a classic situation for an Avoidance Play.

Declarer's first move must be to duck the opening lead so that East has no possibility of getting the lead in hearts. Say that West continues with a second heart. Declarer wins and leads a trump off the dummy. Whatever card East plays, cover it as cheaply as possible. If East played the five or eight,

West will usually win the trick, after which declarer cashes the top trumps as soon as he regains the lead. If East played an honour on the first spade lead, declarer wins and crosses to dummy in clubs to lead a second trump. Again he covers East's card as cheaply as possible. By playing this way East can be kept off lead on all three-two breaks unless he holds all three missing honours.

## Points to Remember

♠ Don't be greedy; be willing to concede a possibly unnecessary trick if that will help to ensure the success of the contract.

♠ When one defender is in a position to attack your vulnerable spot and the other is not, try to lose the lead only to the defender who cannot hurt you, even if that means sometimes playing against the theoretical odds in a suit.

♠ When you see the opportunity for an avoidance play, make sure that you leave no loophole for the defence. Often this may simply mean ducking, or covering, the opening lead.

# Try it Yourself

In each case you are declarer, sitting South. How should you play to give yourself the best possible chance to make your contract?

### Question 1

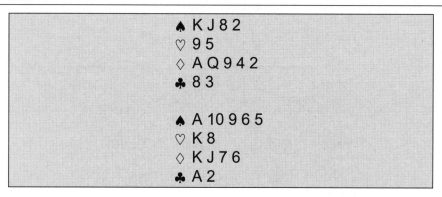

♠ K J 8 2
♡ 9 5
◇ A Q 9 4 2
♣ 8 3

♠ A 10 9 6 5
♡ K 8
◇ K J 7 6
♣ A 2

| West | North | East | South |
|------|-------|------|-------|
| 1♡ | Pass | Pass | 1♠ |
| Pass | 3♠ | Pass | 4♠ |
| All Pass | | | |

The opening lead is the king of clubs, East following with the jack.

### Question 2

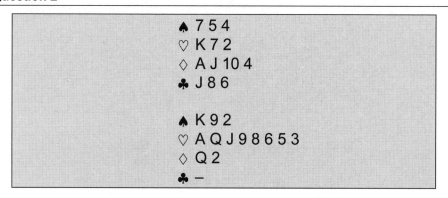

♠ 7 5 4
♡ K 7 2
◇ A J 10 4
♣ J 8 6

♠ K 9 2
♡ A Q J 9 8 6 5 3
◇ Q 2
♣ —

| West | North | East | South |
|------|-------|------|-------|
| | | | 4♡ |
| All Pass | | | |

West leads the ace of clubs.

## Question 3

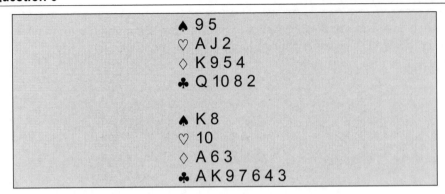

♠ 9 5
♡ A J 2
◇ K 9 5 4
♣ Q 10 8 2

♠ K 8
♡ 10
◇ A 6 3
♣ A K 9 7 6 4 3

| West | North | East | South |
|------|-------|------|-------|
|      |       |      | 1♣    |
| 1♠   | 3♣    | 4♠   | 5♣    |
| All Pass |    |      |       |

West leads the king of hearts.

## Question 4

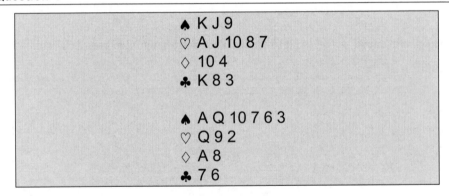

♠ K J 9
♡ A J 10 8 7
◇ 10 4
♣ K 8 3

♠ A Q 10 7 6 3
♡ Q 9 2
◇ A 8
♣ 7 6

| West | North | East | South |
|------|-------|------|-------|
|      | 1♡    | 2◇   | 2♠    |
| Pass | 3♠    | Pass | 4♠    |
| All Pass |   |      |       |

The opening lead is the three of diamonds to East's king.

## Question 5

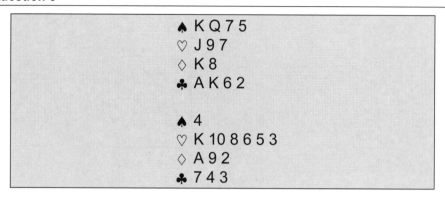

♠ K Q 7 5
♡ J 9 7
◇ K 8
♣ A K 6 2

♠ 4
♡ K 10 8 6 5 3
◇ A 9 2
♣ 7 4 3

| West | North | East | South |
|------|-------|------|-------|
|      | 1NT(i) | Pass | 4♡ |
| All Pass | | | |

(i) 15-17

West leads the jack of spades.

## Question 6

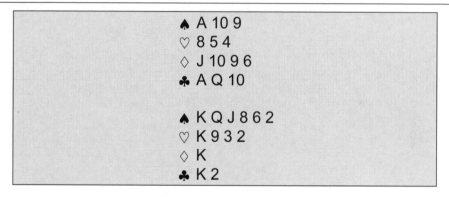

♠ A 10 9
♡ 8 5 4
◇ J 10 9 6
♣ A Q 10

♠ K Q J 8 6 2
♡ K 9 3 2
◇ K
♣ K 2

| West | North | East | South |
|------|-------|------|-------|
|      |       |      | 1♠ |
| Pass | 2◇ | Pass | 2♡ |
| Pass | 3♠ | Pass | 4♠ |
| All Pass | | | |

The opening lead is the three of clubs.

## Question 7

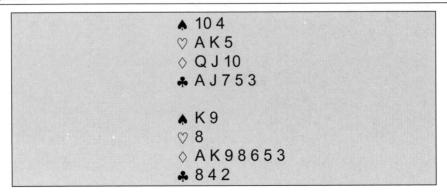

♠ 10 4
♡ A K 5
◇ Q J 10
♣ A J 7 5 3

♠ K 9
♡ 8
◇ A K 9 8 6 5 3
♣ 8 4 2

| West | North | East | South |
|------|-------|------|-------|
| 1♡ | 1NT | Pass | 3◇ |
| Pass | 4◇ | Pass | 4♡ |
| Pass | 5◇ | All Pass | |

The lead is the queen of hearts.

## Question 8

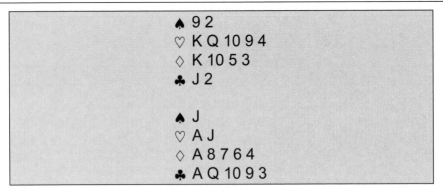

♠ 9 2
♡ K Q 10 9 4
◇ K 10 5 3
♣ J 2

♠ J
♡ A J
◇ A 8 7 6 4
♣ A Q 10 9 3

| West | North | East | South |
|------|-------|------|-------|
| | | | 1◇ |
| Pass | 1♡ | 1♠ | 2♣ |
| 3♠ | 4◇ | Pass | 5◇ |
| All Pass | | | |

West leads ace then a low spade.

## Question 9

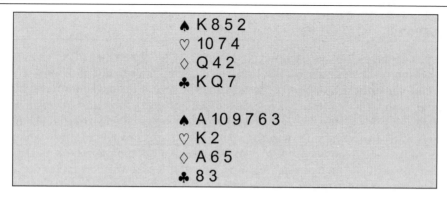

♠ K 8 5 2
♡ 10 7 4
◇ Q 4 2
♣ K Q 7

♠ A 10 9 7 6 3
♡ K 2
◇ A 6 5
♣ 8 3

| West | North | East | South |
|------|-------|------|-------|
| 1♣ | Pass | 1♡ | 1♠ |
| 2♡ | 3♠ | All Pass | |

West leads the jack of diamonds.

## Question 10

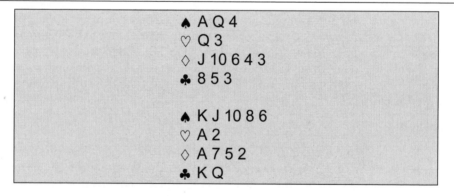

♠ A Q 4
♡ Q 3
◇ J 10 6 4 3
♣ 8 5 3

♠ K J 10 8 6
♡ A 2
◇ A 7 5 2
♣ K Q

| West | North | East | South |
|------|-------|------|-------|
| | | | 1♠ |
| 2♡ | 2♠ | 3♡ | 4♠ |
| All Pass | | | |

West leads the nine of diamonds.

# Solutions

## Question 1

Even if declarer loses a trick to the queen of spades, he will still have at least ten winners. The danger is that he loses a spade, a club and two hearts. That can happen only if East gains the lead and pushes a heart through the king. Declarer should therefore play spades by cashing the king and taking a second-round finesse into the safe West hand. However, to ensure that West cannot hurt him if he does win the spade queen, declarer must first make sure that there is no way in which West can give his partner the lead. Declarer must duck the opening lead and can then make the recommended play in the trump suit to ensure his contract.

## Question 2

The only danger to this contract is that a losing diamond finesse might see East switch to a spade honour and the defence take three more tricks in that suit. If the South hand contained only a singleton queen of diamonds, there would be a safe alternative, namely a ruffing diamond finesse, using the jack and ten to create the tenth trick. If West wins a diamond trick he cannot fruitfully attack the spade weak spot.

It is difficult to see unless one is familiar with the concept of avoidance play, but there is a way in which declarer can reduce his holding to bare queen of diamonds. All he has to do is to discard the small diamond on the ace of clubs! West can do nothing to threaten the contract at this point and as soon as declarer gains the lead he can draw trumps and take the ruffing finesse to ensure his contract.

## Question 3

After East-West have bid and supported spades, it is almost a certainty that the ace will be sitting over the king. If not, why has West not led the partnership suit? The only chance for the contract would appear to be a three-three diamond split, which would enable declarer to discard one of his spade losers on the thirteenth diamond. The difficulty is that the diamonds must be established without allowing East to gain the lead to play a spade through the king.

Declarer should duck the opening lead, despite holding a singleton facing the ace. He wins the next trick and draws trumps, then pitches a diamond on the ace of hearts. Now declarer is in a position to play three rounds of diamonds, ruffing in hand. If the suit breaks three-three, he crosses to dummy and takes his discard. If the diamonds do not divide evenly, the only hope is the very slim chance that the spade ace is onside after all.

## Question 4

If the heart finesse works there will be no fewer than twelve tricks to be taken. If it loses, however, there is a danger of losing a heart, a diamond and two club tricks if the club ace is also offside – quite likely after East's over-call.

There can be two club losers only if West gets in to lead through the king, otherwise declarer's clubs will eventually be disposed of on the hearts. It would be wrong to win the first trick as this would run the risk of a losing heart finesse and East playing a diamond to his partner's queen for the club play. Simply duck the king of diamonds. East is powerless. As soon as de-clarer gains the lead he draws trumps and runs the nine then queen of hearts, not minding if East wins the king, as the club position is still pro-tected.

## Question 5

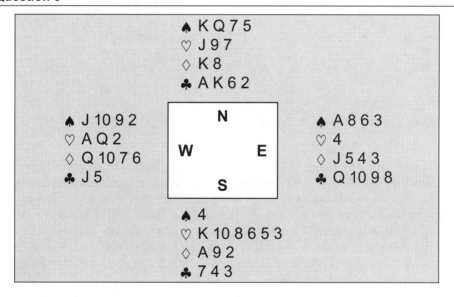

Nine players out of ten would cover the opening lead and feel aggrieved when their contract went down when the cards were as in the diagram. Indeed, they would probably not realise that they had misplayed and so gone down in a cold contract. The danger is that East can win the spade ace and switch to a small singleton trump, West playing three rounds. That puts paid to any hope of ruffing the third diamond in dummy and the only remaining chance is that clubs divide evenly, the thirteenth card becoming declarer's tenth trick.

The diamond ruff can be prevented only if East gains the lead. Declarer should duck the jack of spades. West can do nothing at this point so declarer will get his diamond ruff. Later, he can lead a spade honour off the table to establish his spade trick for the necessary club discard, the ace and king of clubs providing the dummy entries to make this play possible. Only a six-two spade split, seven-one diamond split or five-one club split will defeat the game.

## Question 6

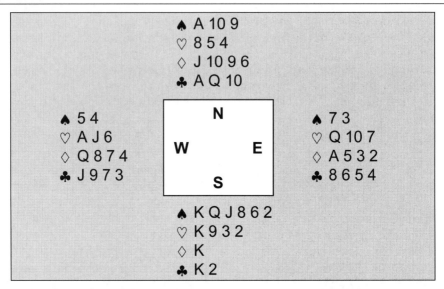

Declarer has nine top tricks and needs one more, either the king of hearts or a diamond trick. The heart is a 50-50 chance, while a combination play in hearts and diamonds looks to be somewhat better. Say that declarer wins the opening lead and plays the king of diamonds. If West holds the ace, he will be unable to attack hearts effectively. Declarer will regain the lead and take the ruffing diamond finesse to establish sufficient winners without risking the heart position. But if it is East who wins the diamond ace a heart switch will threaten the contract's success.

The combination play is around 75%, as it succeeds whenever West has the diamond ace or East has the heart ace. Not bad, but there is something better still.

The opening lead looks like fourth best, so three rounds of clubs should stand up. On the third round, declarer throws the king of diamonds. Now he runs the jack of diamonds, throwing a heart if East has played low. If West wins this trick he cannot afford to lead hearts so will exit with a trump. Declarer wins in dummy and leads the ten of diamonds, again discarding a heart if East plays low. Though West may hold both diamond honours, the nine is now established for a third heart and the defence can come to only one heart trick.

## Question 7

The ace of spades is probably in the West hand. To succeed, declarer will have to establish the clubs without allowing East to gain the lead. The best way to achieve this is to duck the opening lead, despite having both ace and king facing a singleton! Declarer can now pitch two clubs on the ace and king of hearts, then play ace and ruff a club high. He can cross twice more to dummy with diamond plays to ruff two more clubs high, so establishes an extra winner even if the suit splits four-one. Finally, he crosses to dummy one last time in trumps and the long club is the eleventh trick. An even club break gives an overtrick, of course.

## Question 8

Declarer ruffs the second spade and plays the ace of diamonds, as he cannot cater to East holding all four trumps. If both defenders follow with small cards a second diamond is played to the king. What if East drops an honour on the first round of diamonds? A second diamond is played and West follows with the remaining small card. Should declarer finesse the ten or rise with the king?

It is not a guess. If West has three trumps the contract is secure even if declarer loses a trump trick to him. The play is the same as if West had turned up with queen, jack and another trump. Declarer goes up with the diamond king and runs the hearts, throwing clubs from hand. Eventually, West either ruffs a heart or is thrown in with his trump after all the hearts have been played. He is endplayed, forced either to lead a club into the ace, queen or give a ruff and discard, on which declarer's final club will be discarded.

If East has the trump trick, or West has all four trumps, the club finesse will be required at some point. Had declarer finessed on the second diamond and this had lost, he would have again required the club finesse.

## Question 9

The first thing to ask is, where is the king of diamonds? Despite the fact that it was West who opened the bidding, the king is surely with East. West would not risk a dangerous lead from a king, jack holding when he could just lead the suit his partner had bid or, failing that, a trump. There is then little point in putting up the queen of diamonds.

On the contrary, that would be precisely the way to risk defeat. The danger is that the defence comes to two diamonds, two hearts and the ace of clubs. If East holds the king of diamonds, that makes West favourite to have the club ace, in which case two club tricks can be established by leading towards dummy's honours twice, and that will create a discard for one of the two heart losers. This will help only if East is kept off lead so that there can never be a heart lead through the vulnerable king.

The solution is to duck the opening lead in both hands and, if West continues with the ten of diamonds, duck that as well. East has now been prevented from gaining the lead in diamonds. When declarer gains the lead he draws trumps and leads a club up, then back to hand with a trump to lead another club up. The defence is powerless.

## Question 10

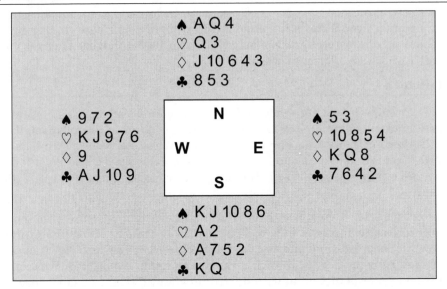

The contract will succeed if declarer can avoid losing two diamonds, a club and a heart. It seems that West holds the heart king so East must be kept off lead until the diamonds can be established for a heart discard. The instinctive play of covering the opening lead will prove to be fatal and anyway can never gain. If the suit is two-two East will have to play an honour and declarer wins the ace, draws trumps and gives up a diamond. If the suit is three-one, East always has two diamond tricks.

To succeed, declarer must avoid East winning the first defensive diamond trick when the suit splits three-one. Correct play is to duck the opening lead in both hands if East follows with the eight. Declarer wins the switch and draws trumps, then plays ace and another diamond, and the heart goes away on the fifth diamond.

# Chapter Eight

# Elimination and Endplay

- ♡ **Improving the Odds**
- ♡ **Points to Remember**
- ♡ **Try it Yourself**

  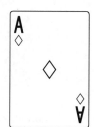 

# Improving the Odds

A finesse is only a 50% proposition and even a double finesse, e.g 5 4 3 facing A J 10, only about 75%. It would be so much better then if declarer could avoid taking the finesse altogether. In the right circumstances it may be possible to force an opponent to lead into our tenace position, guaranteeing success. In other words, we Endplay him. An endplay will work only if we can first Eliminate all the defenders' safe options in the other suits.

There are many suit combinations that lend themselves to elimination and endplay, including the following:

| | | | | |
|---|---|---|---|---|
| (i) | A J 10 | facing | 4 3 2 | needing two tricks |
| (ii) | A Q 9 | facing | 4 3 2 | needing two tricks |
| (iii) | A J 7 | facing | K 10 6 | needing three tricks |
| (iv) | J 9 2 | facing | Q 8 3 | needing one trick |
| (v) | K J 2 | facing | 6 5 4 | needing one trick |
| (vi) | K 10 2 | facing | 6 5 4 | needing one trick |
| (vii) | Q J 2 | facing | 6 5 4 | needing one trick |
| (viii) | A J 2 | facing | 10 5 3 | needing two tricks |
| (ix) | A 10 2 | facing | K 9 6 | needing three tricks |
| (x) | A J 9 | facing | 5 4 3 | needing two tricks |

In cases (i) to (viii) a perfect elimination and endplay will guarantee success, while in the last two cases it will greatly improve declarer's chances, but without any guarantees.

Let's see how this technique might work in a complete hand.

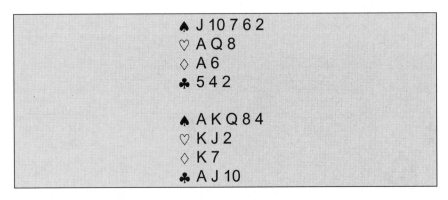

♠ J 10 7 6 2
♡ A Q 8
◇ A 6
♣ 5 4 2

♠ A K Q 8 4
♡ K J 2
◇ K 7
♣ A J 10

Declarer plays in Six Spades on the lead of the queen of diamonds. After winning and drawing trumps, the only problem is in the club suit. The double finesse will succeed three times in four, but why take the risk that both missing honours are over the ace? Draw trumps and cash all the red winners, ending in the North hand. Now play a club to the ten. It doesn't matter if this finesse loses because look at West's options; all his safe exit cards have been eliminated so he is endplayed. If he returns another club, it is into the ace, jack, and no further finesse will be required. If West returns a red card, declarer can ruff in one hand and discard a club from the other. Again, there is no need for a second finesse. The 75% chance has become 100% thanks to the elimination and endplay.

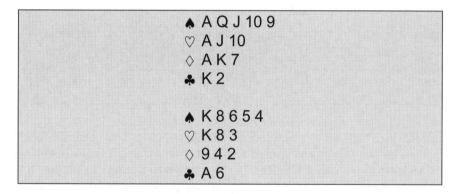

Again the contract is Six Spades, this time on the lead of the jack of clubs. The contract appears to be on the two-way heart guess but, of course, that guess can be avoided. Declarer wins the opening lead, draws the missing trumps, cashes the other club winner then plays three rounds of diamonds. Whichever defender wins this trick has the choice of leading a heart, finding the queen for declarer, or of giving a ruff and discard, so that the heart guess is no longer required.

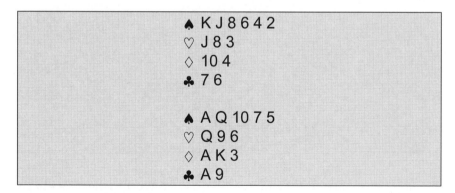

Four Spades now, and the lead is the queen of clubs. Left to himself, declarer has the problem of how to play the hearts for one winner and only two losers.

But if he is familiar with elimination and endplay technique the hand is a sure thing. He wins the opening lead and draws trumps. Next he plays three rounds of diamonds, ruffing the third round, then exits with his club loser. Whoever wins this trick must either give a ruff and discard or open up the hearts, either of which presents declarer with the contract.

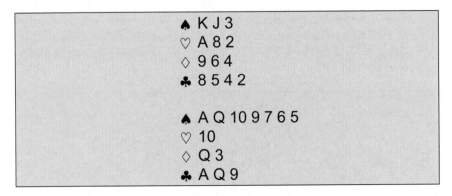

♠ K J 3
♡ A 8 2
◊ 9 6 4
♣ 8 5 4 2

♠ A Q 10 9 7 6 5
♡ 10
◊ Q 3
♣ A Q 9

Again the contract is Four Spades and West leads ace, king and a third diamond, declarer ruffing. The contract will be a sure thing if trumps split two-one. Declarer plays ace and ruffs a heart, crosses to dummy in trumps and ruffs the last heart. Now he crosses to dummy's other top trump and leads a club, covering East's card as cheaply as possible. With every suit eliminated, West can win this trick but is endplayed. If he returns a club, it is into declarer's tenace, while a ruff and discard allows a ruff in dummy and a club discard from hand. This is why the even trump split was needed. There would be no ruff and discard if three rounds were needed to draw the missing trumps, as dummy would not be able to ruff a red-suit return.

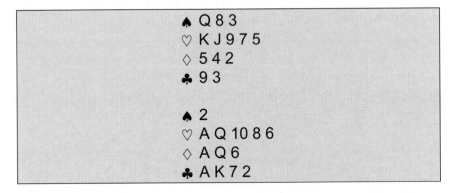

♠ Q 8 3
♡ K J 9 7 5
◊ 5 4 2
♣ 9 3

♠ 2
♡ A Q 10 8 6
◊ A Q 6
♣ A K 7 2

A slam hunt stops just in time in Five Hearts and West cashes the king of spades then, reading the position accurately, switches to a trump, East following. On the reasonable assumption that West holds the ace of spades, the diamond finesse is not required. Declarer draws the remaining trump and plays three rounds of clubs, ruffing. Next comes a ruff of the low spade, followed by another club ruff. The elimination is complete. Declarer leads the queen of spades and, when East follows low, pitches his low diamond. West can win but is endplayed; either he leads into the ace, queen of diamonds or he gives a ruff and discard. Once again, a perfect elimination and endplay turns an even-money proposition into a sure thing.

The key to all of these situations is that the elimination must be done to leave an opponent with no safe exit card before he is put on lead. If there is no elimination, there is no endplay, as he will have a safe escape route.

## Points to Remember

♠ Finesses, by their very nature, offer no guarantee of success. However, if an opponent can be endplayed and forced to lead into your tenace, then success may be assured.

♠ For an endplay to succeed, it is first essential to eliminate all the defender's safe exit cards so that he is obliged to do what is required of him.

♠ Generally, the eventual endplay will only succeed if declarer and dummy both still have trumps left at the point where the endplay is performed, otherwise the defender will often have a safe exit card, as there can be no ruff and discard if declarer has no option as to where to ruff.

# Try it Yourself

In each case you are declarer, sitting South. How should you play to give yourself the best possible chance to make your contract?

## Question 1

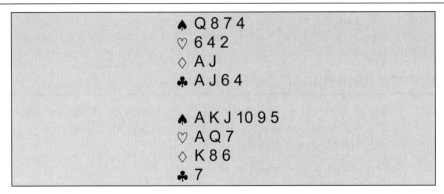

| West | North | East | South |
|------|-------|------|-------|
|      |       |      | 2♠    |
| Pass | 3♠    | Pass | 4♡    |
| Pass | 4NT   | Pass | 5♡    |
| Pass | 5NT   | Pass | 6♡    |
| Pass | 6♠    | All Pass |    |

West leads the king of clubs.

## Question 2

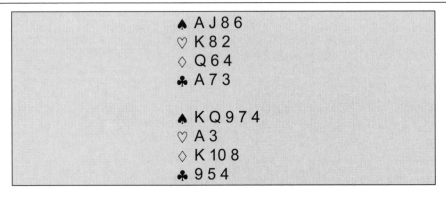

| West | North | East | South |
|------|-------|------|-------|
|      |       |      | 1♠    |
| 2♣   | 4♠    | All Pass |    |

The opening lead is the king of clubs.

## Question 3

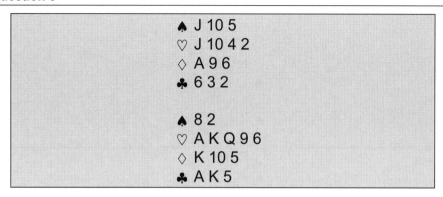

♠ J 10 5
♡ J 10 4 2
◊ A 9 6
♣ 6 3 2

♠ 8 2
♡ A K Q 9 6
◊ K 10 5
♣ A K 5

| West | North | East | South |
|------|-------|------|-------|
|      |       |      | 1♡    |
| Pass | 2♡    | Pass | 4♡    |
| All Pass | | | |

West leads the ace, king and queen of spades.

## Question 4

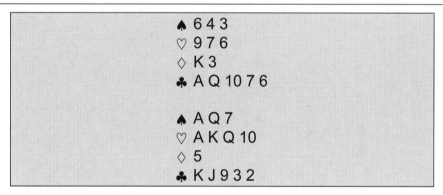

♠ 6 4 3
♡ 9 7 6
◊ K 3
♣ A Q 10 7 6

♠ A Q 7
♡ A K Q 10
◊ 5
♣ K J 9 3 2

| West | North | East | South |
|------|-------|------|-------|
|      |       |      | 1♣    |
| 1◊   | 3♣    | 3◊   | 4◊    |
| Pass | 5♣    | All Pass | |

West leads the queen of diamonds.

## Question 5

♠ 8 6 4 2
♡ K Q 7 3
◇ K 7
♣ Q 9 5

♠ J 7
♡ A J 10 6 2
◇ A 9 5
♣ A 7 3

| West | North | East | South |
|------|-------|------|-------|
|      |       | 1♠   | 2♡    |
| Pass | 4♡    | All Pass |   |

West leads the ten of spades to East's king. East continues with the ace then queen of spades. Trumps prove to be two-two.

## Question 6

♠ K 10 8 7 6
♡ 9 7 4
◇ J 8
♣ K Q J

♠ A Q J 5 2
♡ A K 3
◇ K 5
♣ 10 8 3

| West | North | East | South |
|------|-------|------|-------|
|      |       |      | 1♠    |
| 2◇   | 3♠    | Pass | 4♠    |
| All Pass |   |      |       |

The opening lead is the queen of hearts.

## Question 7

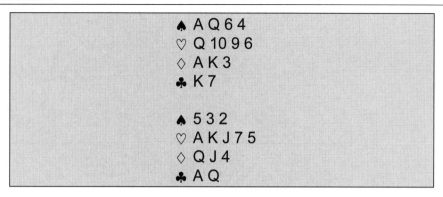

♠ A Q 6 4
♡ Q 10 9 6
◇ A K 3
♣ K 7

♠ 5 3 2
♡ A K J 7 5
◇ Q J 4
♣ A Q

| West | North | East | South |
|------|-------|------|-------|
|      |       |      | 1♡    |
| Pass | 1♠    | Pass | 2NT   |
| Pass | 3♡    | Pass | 4♡    |
| Pass | 6♡    | All Pass | |

West leads the ten of diamonds.

## Question 8

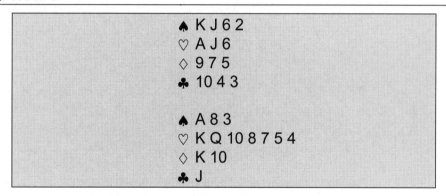

♠ K J 6 2
♡ A J 6
◇ 9 7 5
♣ 10 4 3

♠ A 8 3
♡ K Q 10 8 7 5 4
◇ K 10
♣ J

| West | North | East | South |
|------|-------|------|-------|
|      |       |      | 1♡    |
| 2♣   | 2♡    | 3♣   | 4♡    |
| All Pass | | | |

West leads the ace then king of clubs. Trumps are two-one, West having the length.

## Question 9

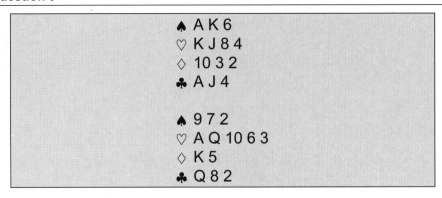

♠ A K 6
♡ K J 8 4
◇ 10 3 2
♣ A J 4

♠ 9 7 2
♡ A Q 10 6 3
◇ K 5
♣ Q 8 2

| West | North | East | South |
|------|-------|------|-------|
| 1◇ | Dble | Pass | 4♡ |
| All Pass | | | |

West leads the queen of spades.

## Question 10

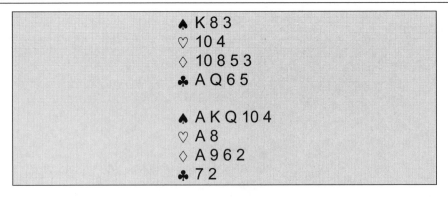

♠ K 8 3
♡ 10 4
◇ 10 8 5 3
♣ A Q 6 5

♠ A K Q 10 4
♡ A 8
◇ A 9 6 2
♣ 7 2

| West | North | East | South |
|------|-------|------|-------|
| | | | 1♠ |
| Pass | 2♠ | Pass | 4♠ |
| All Pass | | | |

The opening lead is the three of hearts to East's king.

# Solutions

## Question 1

There are possible finesses in both red suits and the success of either one could make declarer's slam. However, one of two finesses will only succeed roughly three-quarters of the time, and there is a better option available, requiring only that West hold the queen of clubs to back up his lead of the king and that the missing trumps split two-one.

The correct line of play is to win the club ace and ruff a club high, preserving the spade five as a possible dummy entry. Now draw trumps ending in dummy. If trumps are two-one, ruff a club then play three rounds of diamonds, ruffing. Finally, play the jack of clubs, discarding the seven of hearts. West wins the king but is endplayed, forced to lead into the heart tenace or give a ruff and discard.

If trumps are three-zero, there will be no trump left in dummy after trumps have been drawn and the diamonds ruffed out, so West will be able to get off play with a diamond in the ending without giving a ruff and discard. After drawing trumps, declarer can still play to ruff out the club king, and if that doesn't work can finesse first the jack of diamonds then the queen of hearts, succeeding when any one of these three chances comes home.

## Question 2

There is a real danger of a six-one club split after West's overcall, so declarer must win the ace immediately. He draws trumps then plays three rounds of hearts, ruffing, to eliminate the defence's safe exit cards. Finally, declarer exits with a club. After taking two club tricks, West must open up the diamonds, guaranteeing the contract. Even if East can win the second club and switch to a diamond (West holding AJ9), the nine forces the queen but now a second club exit endplays West.

## Question 3

With a sure club loser to come, declarer must avoid losing a diamond if the contract is to succeed. He ruffs the third spade and draws trumps, then plays three rounds of clubs, forcing whoever wins the third round to open up the diamonds. There are no guarantees from here but declarer has good chances.

If the defenders switch to a low diamond, the next hand plays low and an honour comes up. Declarer now finesses against the remaining honour on the way back and succeeds when the honours were split. If instead they switch to a diamond honour, declarer has to judge whether this is from queen, jack or the honours are split.

Against good defenders, the defence could often have chosen who won the third club. If one defender held both diamond honours, they would have tried to let his partner win the third club. If the hand with only small diamonds opens up the suit, the defence will normally come to a trick. So declarer should still play for split honours, playing for his opponents to have defended accurately, unless it is clear that the defenders had no choice in clubs.

## Question 4

There is a diamond to lose and one or two spades. The ace of diamonds is presumably offside, so there is little point in covering with the king, which may see East win and make an unwelcome spade switch. Declarer plays low and West is likely to play a second diamond, ruffed. Declarer draws trumps in two rounds and cashes the ace and king of hearts. The jack does not appear. Declarer crosses to dummy with a trump and leads the third heart, East following low. Should he finesse or play for the drop?

Simply looking at the odds, it is a close call which play is correct, but looking at the whole hand there is one clearly correct play and one clearly incorrect play. If declarer puts up the queen and finds that East began with jack to four, he will be left reliant on the spade finesse – a poor prospect on the auction. However, if he takes the finesse he will have a discard from dummy when it wins. And if the ten loses to the jack? Then West will be endplayed, forced to lead into the spade tenace or give a ruff and discard. With one of dummy's spades going on the queen of hearts, that is good enough for the contract.

## Question 5

Declarer must ruff the third spade high or risk an over-ruff and swift defeat. He draws trumps in two rounds, then plays king, ace and ruffs the last diamond. There is just room for West to hold the king of clubs, but the likelihood is that it is with East, suggesting that an endplay may be required.

The best chance for success is to lead dummy's last spade, forcing East to cover, and discard a low club from hand. Either East gives a ruff and discard or he opens up the clubs. If he has the club king this is fatal to the defence. Of course, if West has the king the contract will fail and declarer will feel foolish, but surely he played with the odds so should not feel so bad.

## Question 6

The ace of diamonds is sure to be sitting over the king, making prospects look distinctly gloomy. However, there is a chance if either West has to win the third heart or East has the diamond queen.

Declarer wins the heart lead and draws trumps, then knocks out the ace of clubs. Winning the heart or club return, declarer cashes the remaining clubs and exits with the third heart. If West wins the trick he is endplayed and the contract is secure. If East wins and leads a low diamond, declarer plays low, hoping that the queen is on his right. If it is, dummy's jack will force West to win the ace and the diamond king will be the tenth trick.

## Question 7

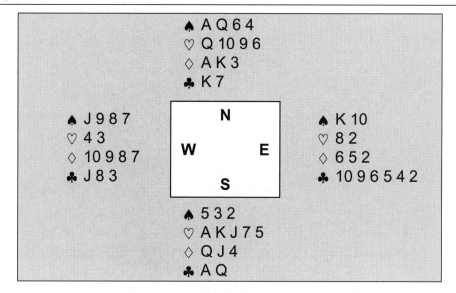

The unfortunate club duplication means that this contract is not as good as could have been expected during the auction. Declarer has to find a way to avoid two spade losers, and his spot cards are too weak for him to expect to be able to duck the first round to East after eliminating the other suits. The opening lead can be won in either hand, then trumps drawn. If the trumps are three-one, declarer should cash the ace of spades then all the minor-suit winners before playing a spade to the queen. If West has the spade king, this is just as effective as taking a first round finesse. The extra chance comes when East has singleton or doubleton king. When he wins the doubleton king he is endplayed, forced to give a ruff and discard.

If trumps are two-two, declarer can try for a small extra chance first. The extra trump means that he can try a low spade from hand without cashing the ace first. If a sleepy West follows with the seven, the smallest missing card, thinking that it makes no difference what he plays from nine, eight, seven, for example, he can be taught the error of his ways. If the seven appears, declarer ducks in dummy, knowing that East is bound to have to overtake, after which he is endplayed. If West does not play the seven, declarer rises with the ace, crosses to hand with a trump, and plays a spade to the queen.

## Question 8

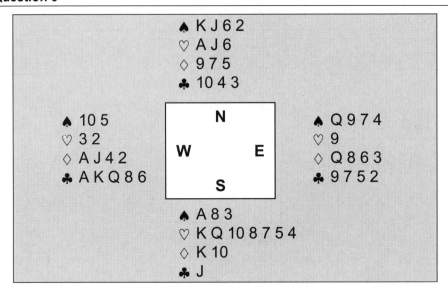

Declarer ruffs the second club and draws trumps in two rounds. Now there is a pretty ending if West holds the queen of clubs. Declarer cashes the ace and king of spades, then plays the club ten. If East plays low, declarer discards his remaining spade. West wins the club and has a choice of losing options. A diamond lead guarantees a trick for the king, while another club would give a ruff and discard. Finally, a spade lead allows declarer to establish a spade trick without risk.

If East turns up with the club queen, declarer ruffs and leads his last spade, hoping to find West holding the queen. The jack of spades will then provide a parking place for a diamond loser.

## Question 9

West is very likely to hold the king of clubs and ace of diamonds, meaning that the club finesse will win but, unless the king is doubleton, there will be a club to lose and two diamonds to go along with the third round of spades. Perhaps an endplay is possible? Declarer wins the spade and draws trumps, then plays a club to the jack, cashes the club ace and remaining top spade, then exits with a club. Alas, West has retained a low spade and leads this to his partner's ten for a diamond lead through the king – down one.

To create an effective endplay, declarer must duck the first trick. Winning the continuation, he draws trumps, takes the club finesse, and cashes the spade and club winners before exiting with the third club. This time there is no escape for West.

## Question 10

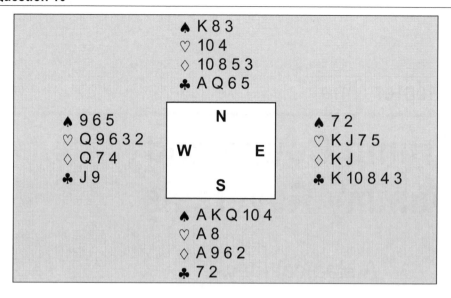

Declarer would appear to require an even diamond break plus the club finesse. With only a five-three trump fit, there can be no perfect elimination and endplay as there will be no trump left in the dummy if all the defensive trumps are drawn. A partial elimination may offer a small extra chance, however.

Declarer must duck the opening lead to cut defensive communications. He wins the second heart and cashes just two rounds of trumps, leaving one outstanding, then plays ace and another diamond. If East began with only two trumps and is forced to win the second diamond, as in the diagram, he will be endplayed. West cannot overtake the second diamond to play a spade through, as that costs his side a diamond trick.

# Chapter Nine

# Trump Coups and Dummy Reversals

- ♡ **A Magical Play?**
- ♡ **Dummy Reversal**
- ♡ **Points to Remember**
- ♡ **Try it Yourself**

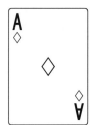

# A Magical Play?

A Trump Coup is, effectively, a way in which declarer can take a trump finesse despite not having a low trump to lead for that finesse. Sounds a little like magic? Not at all; sometimes the required trump finesse can be taken by leading a card in a side suit, or perhaps even by forcing the opposition to lead to your advantage. Say that this is the endgame in a spade contract:

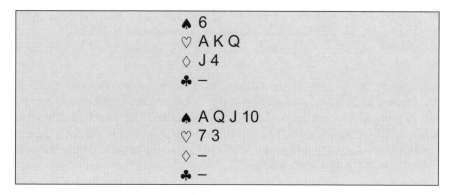

Declarer is in dummy and leads low to the ten of spades. West shows out, marking East with king to three spades; in other words, though the finesse succeeded, East still holds king doubleton trump and there is no small spade left in dummy to repeat the finesse. Suppose that declarer simply cashes the ace and king of hearts then ruffs a red card. That will leave him in hand with ace, queen doubleton spade. Inevitably, East will come to a trick with his remaining king doubleton.

Now suppose that declarer is familiar with the technique of the trump coup. Instead of cashing two top hearts, he plays a heart to the ace then ruffs a diamond. That shortens his trumps to the same length as East, two each. A second heart is played to dummy and, with only two cards remaining in each hand, any red card is led. Declarer waits to see East's play then over-ruffs him as cheaply as possible. The lead of the side suit card has allowed the trump finesse to be taken. The key to success was the trump reduction play, when declarer ruffed the diamond to bring his own trump length down to the same as his opponent's.

In the following example, the contract is Six Spades and West leads the jack of clubs. Declarer wins in hand with the king and lays down the ace and king of trumps, only to see West discard a diamond on the second round. With an inescapable diamond loser, declarer must find a way to pick up East's trump holding without loss, which will require a trump coup.

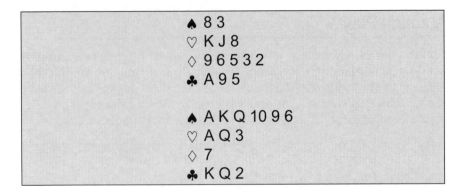

At trick four, declarer gives up a diamond. East wins and returns a club, which is won with dummy's ace and a diamond ruffed. Declarer cashes the queen of clubs then crosses to the jack of hearts to take a second diamond ruff. Now his trumps are the same length as East's. The remaining hearts are cashed, ending in dummy. At trick twelve, a diamond lead permits declarer to trap East's jack of spades.

This play needed some good fortune as both three rounds of clubs and three rounds of hearts had to stand up, as otherwise East would have ruffed in before the trump coup had been established, but it was the only chance.

## Dummy Reversal

The Dummy Reversal is a very different technique but one which once again attempts to make the best use of declarer's combined trump holding to produce the maximum number of tricks. Generally, we are taught that we should attempt to take ruffs in the shorter trump hand as this produces extra tricks, where ruffing in the long trump hand may merely be a different way of cashing winners that declarer already has, so does not produce any extra tricks. However, sometimes it is possible to do a lot of ruffing in the long trump hand then draw trumps using the shorter hand. Take this example:

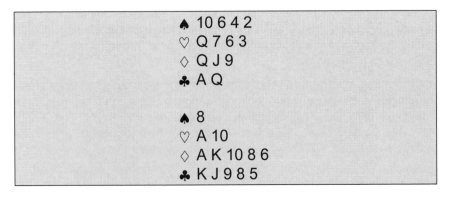

Playing in Six Diamonds on the lead of ace then king of spades, straightforward play would appear to produce only eleven tricks, five in each minor plus the heart ace. But declarer has been obliged to ruff in the long trump hand at trick two. Suppose that he could take two more ruffs in that hand and draw trumps with dummy's queen, jack, nine. Would he not then have three trump tricks, three ruffs, five clubs and the ace of hearts – twelve in all?

The play is to take the ruff at trick two with the trump ace, lead low to the diamond queen and ruff another spade with the king of trumps, then lead South's last trump to dummy. Assuming the necessary three-two trump split, dummy's last trump now draws the defenders' last trump, the clubs are unblocked, and declarer crosses to the ace of hearts to cash the rest of the clubs for twelve tricks!

The key to a successful dummy reversal play is that dummy must have strong trumps and sufficient entries to both take the ruffs in hand and get back to draw the last trump. It would be easy to overlook this next example because there appears to be a more straightforward line available.

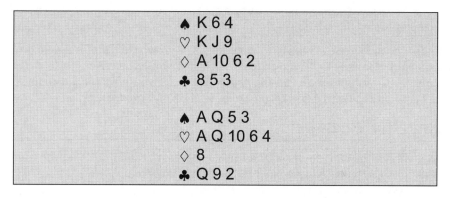

The contract is Four Hearts and West kicks off with a low club to the ace. Back comes another club and the queen loses to the king. West cashes the jack of clubs then switches to a diamond. It may seem that the contract depends on a three-three spade split, with perhaps the extra chance of cashing two rounds of trumps then trying four rounds of spades, making if the same hand has four spades and three hearts. But the dummy reversal offers substantially better odds.

Win the diamond ace and ruff a diamond high. Play a heart to dummy, ruff a diamond high and play another heart to dummy. A third diamond ruff is followed by a spade to the king and the last trump is drawn. This line requires a three-two trump break, about a 68% chance, as opposed to the 35.5% chance of an even spade break.

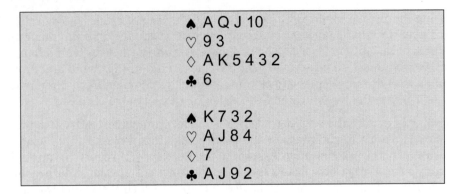

♠ A Q J 10
♡ 9 3
◇ A K 5 4 3 2
♣ 6

♠ K 7 3 2
♡ A J 8 4
◇ 7
♣ A J 9 2

South plays in Six Spades on the lead of the king of hearts. With poor trump spots in hand, it looks right to reverse the dummy – take ruffs in hand to establish the diamonds, then use dummy's powerful spades to draw trumps. Win the heart and play a diamond to the ace, then ruff a diamond low. Next, lead a low spade to dummy and ruff another diamond with the king. Declarer's last trump can be led to dummy, the remaining trumps drawn and the diamonds cashed.

This line of play requires only that spades are no worse than four-one and diamonds no worse than four-two. Note that it would be wrong to cash the second top diamond before taking the ruffs. That would increase the danger that West might be in a position to over-ruff on the next round.

# Points to Remember

♠ It is sometimes possible to finesse against a defender's trump holding despite not having a card in the trump suit facing your tenace. This is known as a trump coup and is effected by leading a side-suit card at the crucial moment.

♠ Careful timing is required to play a trump coup effectively, often involving preparatory work such as taking earlier ruffs to shorten one's trump holding.

♠ If sufficient ruffs can be taken in the long trump hand, and the opposing trumps eventually drawn by the short trump hand, extra tricks can sometimes be made via a dummy reversal, as this technique is known.

♠ The key to a successful dummy reversal is normally that the short trump holding must be strong and that there must be adequate communications between the two hands.

# Try it Yourself

In each case you are declarer, sitting South. How should you play to give yourself the best possible chance to make your contract?

### Question 1

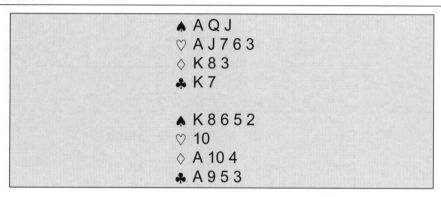

♠ A Q J
♡ A J 7 6 3
◇ K 8 3
♣ K 7

♠ K 8 6 5 2
♡ 10
◇ A 10 4
♣ A 9 5 3

| West | North | East | South |
|------|-------|------|-------|
|      |       |      | 1♠ |
| Pass | 2♡ | Pass | 2♠ |
| Pass | 4NT | Pass | 5♡ |
| Pass | 6♠ | All Pass | |

The opening lead is the king of hearts.

### Question 2

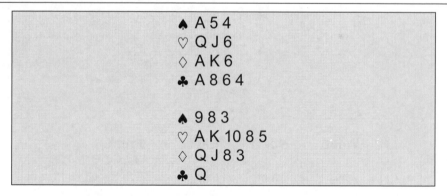

♠ A 5 4
♡ Q J 6
◇ A K 6
♣ A 8 6 4

♠ 9 8 3
♡ A K 10 8 5
◇ Q J 8 3
♣ Q

| West | North | East | South |
|------|-------|------|-------|
|      | 1♣ | Pass | 1♡ |
| Pass | 2NT | Pass | 3◇ |
| Pass | 4♡ | Pass | 4NT |
| Pass | 5♠ | Pass | 6♡ |
| All Pass | | | |

West leads the queen of spades.

## Question 3

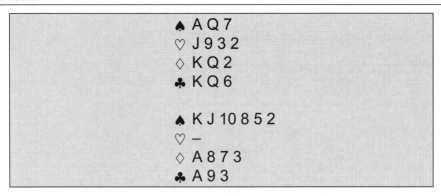

♠ 8 5 2
♡ A 10 4 2
◇ J 3
♣ A J 10 5

♠ A 9 7 6 3
♡ Q
◇ A 8 2
♣ K Q 6 4

| West | North | East | South |
|------|-------|------|-------|
|      |       |      | 1♠    |
| Pass | 2♣    | Pass | 3♣    |
| Pass | 3♠    | Pass | 4♠    |
| All Pass | | | |

The opening lead is the king of spades.

## Question 4

♠ A Q 7
♡ J 9 3 2
◇ K Q 2
♣ K Q 6

♠ K J 10 8 5 2
♡ —
◇ A 8 7 3
♣ A 9 3

| West | North | East | South |
|------|-------|------|-------|
|      |       |      | 1♠    |
| Pass | 2♣    | Pass | 2◇    |
| Pass | 2♡    | Pass | 3♣    |
| Pass | 3♠    | Pass | 4♡    |
| Pass | 4NT   | Pass | 6♡ (i) |
| Pass | 7♠    | All Pass | |

(i) Two aces plus a void

West leads the four of spades to dummy's seven, East following with the three.

## Question 5

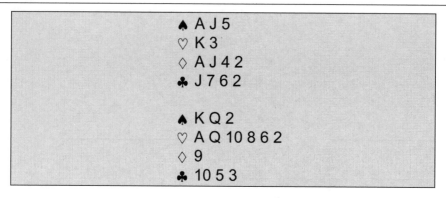

|  | ♠ A J 5 |
|  | ♡ K 3 |
|  | ◊ A J 4 2 |
|  | ♣ J 7 6 2 |
|  | ♠ K Q 2 |
|  | ♡ A Q 10 8 6 2 |
|  | ◊ 9 |
|  | ♣ 10 5 3 |

| West | North | East | South |
|------|-------|------|-------|
|  |  |  | 1♡ |
| 2◊ | 3NT | Pass | 4♡ |
| All Pass |  |  |  |

West cashes the ace, king and queen of clubs, East following throughout, then switches to a low diamond. Play on.

## Question 6

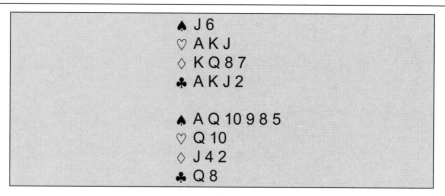

|  | ♠ J 6 |
|  | ♡ A K J |
|  | ◊ K Q 8 7 |
|  | ♣ A K J 2 |
|  | ♠ A Q 10 9 8 5 |
|  | ♡ Q 10 |
|  | ◊ J 4 2 |
|  | ♣ Q 8 |

| West | North | East | South |
|------|-------|------|-------|
|  |  |  | 1♠ |
| Pass | 2♣ | Pass | 2♠ |
| Pass | 3◊ | Pass | 3♠ |
| Pass | 4NT | Pass | 5◊ |
| Pass | 6♠ | All Pass |  |

West cashes the ace of diamonds then leads the eight of hearts.

## Question 7

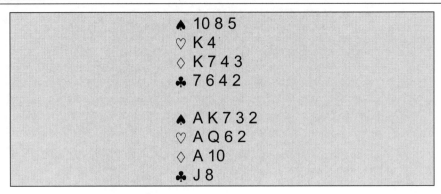

♠ 10 8 5
♡ K 4
♢ K 7 4 3
♣ 7 6 4 2

♠ A K 7 3 2
♡ A Q 6 2
♢ A 10
♣ J 8

| West | North | East | South |
|------|-------|------|-------|
|      |       |      | 1♠    |
| Pass | 2♠    | Pass | 4♠    |
| All Pass |   |      |       |

West leads the ace, king and queen of clubs. Declarer ruffs and cashes the top spades, East turning up with the singleton queen. Play on.

## Question 8

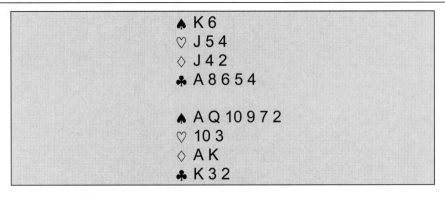

♠ K 6
♡ J 5 4
♢ J 4 2
♣ A 8 6 5 4

♠ A Q 10 9 7 2
♡ 10 3
♢ A K
♣ K 3 2

| West | North | East | South |
|------|-------|------|-------|
|      |       |      | 1♠    |
| Pass | 2♣    | Pass | 3♠    |
| Pass | 4♠    | All Pass |   |

West leads the top three hearts, East following each time and declarer ruffing the third round. When declarer cashes the king and ace of spades he finds that East began with jack to four. Play on.

## Question 9

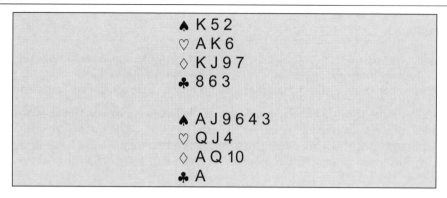

♠ K 5 2
♡ A K 6
◊ K J 9 7
♣ 8 6 3

♠ A J 9 6 4 3
♡ Q J 4
◊ A Q 10
♣ A

| West | North | East | South |
|------|-------|------|-------|
|      |       |      | 1♠    |
| Pass | 3NT   | Pass | 6♠    |
| All Pass |   |      |       |

The opening lead is the queen of clubs. When declarer cashes the ace of spades East shows out.

## Question 10

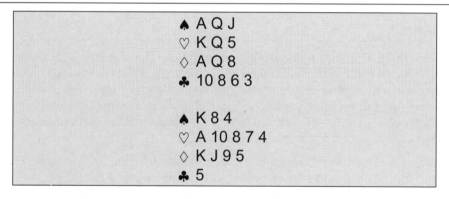

♠ A Q J
♡ K Q 5
◊ A Q 8
♣ 10 8 6 3

♠ K 8 4
♡ A 10 8 7 4
◊ K J 9 5
♣ 5

| West | North | East | South |
|------|-------|------|-------|
|      |       |      | 1♡    |
| 4♣   | 6♡    | All Pass |    |

West leads the king of clubs to East's ace. East switches to the four of diamonds. When declarer cashes the king of hearts, West discards a club. Play on.

# Solutions

## Question 1

To play for two club ruffs in the dummy would require someone to hold ten, nine doubleton spade, as there is an almost certain diamond loser. That is a poor chance, and a dummy reversal looks a much more attractive proposition.

Declarer wins the ace of hearts and ruffs a heart low, crosses to the jack of spades and ruffs another heart low. Another spade to the queen permits a third heart ruff, this time with the king. If the two major suits have divided evenly, declarer needs only to cross to a minor-suit king, draw the last trump and cash the long heart.

## Question 2

Straightforward play offers the prospect of only eleven tricks. However, if declarer could take three club ruffs in hand he would have six trump winners and twelve tricks in all. Declarer wins the opening lead and plays ace of clubs and ruffs a club high. Next he plays ace of hearts and a heart to dummy and ruffs another club high. A diamond to dummy allows declarer to ruff the last club and a second diamond sees him back in dummy to draw the outstanding trump. There are two diamond tricks to come and the dummy reversal makes the slam as long as trumps are three-two and neither of the ace and king of diamonds gets ruffed.

## Question 3

Unless the trumps are blocked, the lead suggests that declarer will not be permitted to ruff his third diamond in the dummy. That leaves four possible losers, even assuming an even trump break, which will surely be essential. However, a dummy reversal might succeed, despite dummy's weak trumps. If declarer can get three heart ruffs in hand, he has four club winners and three other aces to bring his total to ten.

Declarer cannot afford the defenders to make their trumps separately, so would like to draw two rounds before embarking on the dummy reversal. The solution is to duck the opening lead. West has to continue with a second trump or declarer will be able to take a diamond ruff in dummy. Declarer wins the second spade and plays ace and ruffs a heart, plays a club to dummy, and takes a second heart ruff. Another club to dummy permits the last heart to be ruffed, and now declarer simply starts to play his winners. Whoever has the missing trump can ruff in whenever they choose to do so, but declarer will have ten tricks.

## Question 4

There are possibilities of four diamond tricks or of a red-suit squeeze, but the dummy reversal is much more secure.

Declarer allows dummy's seven to win the first trick and ruffs a heart. A spade is led to dummy and a second heart ruffed. Declarer crosses to dummy once in clubs and once in diamonds to take two more heart ruffs. Now he just needs to get back to dummy to draw the outstanding trump, should there be one. If the defender with the last trump has had no opportunity to discard while declarer was taking his heart ruffs, it would be normal to attempt to cross to dummy with a club, as there is less likelihood of an adverse ruff in the suit where the combined holding is six cards in length as opposed to seven in diamonds.

## Question 5

If trumps split three-two there will be no problem, while if West holds jack to four there will be no hope. So declarer should address himself to the possibility that East might hold jack to four trumps. If he wins the ace of diamonds then plays king of hearts and a heart to the ace, it will be too late for a trump coup. There are two dummy entries to allow two diamonds to be ruffed for the necessary trump reduction play, but no third entry to put the lead in dummy at trick twelve for the trump coup itself.

Best is for declarer to simply take a diamond ruff at trick four, just in case. Now he can cash two top hearts and, should East turn up with the awkward jack to four, cross to the jack of spades to ruff a second diamond. There is no need to rely on East's holding three spades; two will do. Declarer plays the queen of spades, overtaking with the ace, and plays the thirteenth club. If East ruffs, declarer over-ruffs, draws the last trump and cashes the king of spades. If East discards on the club, declarer throws the king of spades and now the lead of either the spade or diamond at trick twelve picks up East's trump holding.

## Question 6

Declarer wins the heart switch in dummy and passes the jack of spades successfully. A spade to the nine also wins but West shows out. Declarer must hope to reduce his trumps to the same length as East's, then lead side suit cards through him until he has to ruff, thereby losing his trump trick.

Declarer plays off the remaining hearts, ruffing the third round despite its being a winner. Then he plays three rounds of clubs, again ruffing the third round. A diamond to dummy is followed by the jack of clubs. If East ruffs, he is over-ruffed and declarer has the rest; if East discards, so does declarer and now a diamond from dummy at trick twelve traps the king of spades.

## Question 7

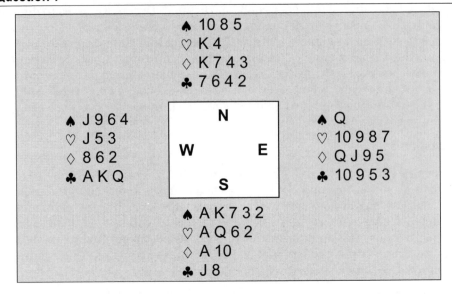

West leads the ace, king and queen of clubs. Declarer ruffs and cashes the top spades, East turning up with the singleton queen. Play on.

Prospects are not good, but there is still a chance despite West's apparent two sure trump tricks. If declarer could arrange to lead a side suit card through West at trick twelve, dummy might then make the ten of spades en passant. That will require West to have just the right distribution, as shown above.

Declarer plays three rounds of diamonds, ruffing in hand, then four rounds of hearts. At trick twelve, the heart lead has the desired effect and West cannot prevent dummy's spade ten from winning.

## Question 8

There is only one entry to dummy, so that a classical trump coup is not possible. However, there is more than one way to skin the proverbial cat. Declarer cashes the ace and king of diamonds, then plays king of clubs and a club to the ace. He ruffs the jack of diamonds, reducing himself to just two trumps, then exits with the club loser. It doesn't matter which defender wins this trick; with someone else on lead at trick twelve, declarer must make the last two trump tricks.

## Question 9

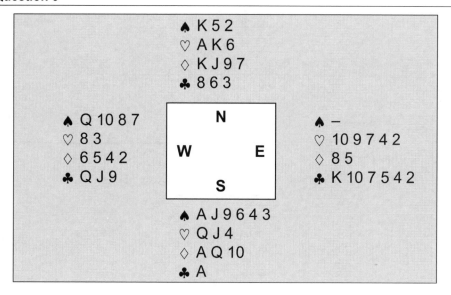

Things do not look good, and a player unfamiliar with the technique of trump reduction might throw in the towel. There is a legitimate chance, however, though it requires West to have the right distribution. Declarer needs to ruff two clubs in hand and cash six red tricks along the way. Having done that he can exit with a low spade and force West to lead into the king, jack at trick twelve.

While West must follow to at least three rounds of diamonds, only two rounds of hearts will be necessary if he actually has four diamonds. Alternatively, it can be three cards in each red suit. To cater to both possibilities, declarer must play three rounds of diamonds before the third heart.

The correct line of play is to cash three rounds of diamonds ending in the dummy, then ruff a club. If West began with four diamonds, cash two hearts and the last diamond then ruff a club; if West began with three diamonds, cash three hearts then ruff a club. If that all has passed off peacefully, exit with the nine of spades and claim the slam.

## Question 10

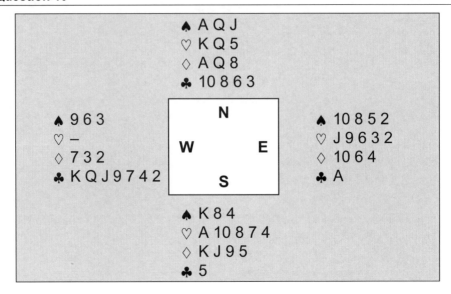

West leads the king of clubs to East's ace. East switches to the four of diamonds. When declarer cashes the king of hearts, West discards a club. Play on.

Though it may look hopeless, there is actually more than one possible layout that permits the slam to be made. If East held four diamonds and three spades, declarer could play queen of hearts and a heart, covering East's card, then cash the seven side winners ending in dummy. A club lead at trick twelve would coup the jack.

However, there is a second chance. Instead of cashing the heart queen, declarer leads the heart five, covering East's card. Next come two rounds of spades and two more rounds of diamonds, ending in dummy. These plays allow declarer to discover East's distribution. If he began with three or four diamonds, declarer cashes the last spade, ruffs a club and ruffs the last diamond with the queen of hearts. That leaves the lead in dummy at trick twelve with the ace and ten of hearts sitting over the jack, nine. If East began with five diamonds, declarer ruffs a club, cashes his last diamond, throwing the club winner from dummy, then ruffs his own club with the queen, and is once again where he needs to be to trap the jack of hearts.

# Chapter Ten

# Squeeze Play

- ♡ **The Positional Squeeze**

- ♡ **The Double Squeeze**

- ♡ **Rectifying the Count**

- ♡ **Points to Remember**

- ♡ **Try it Yourself**

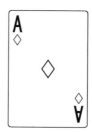

# The Positional Squeeze

A Squeeze occurs when a defender is left with sole control of two suits and cannot keep sufficient cards to do the job effectively. There are many kinds of squeeze and only the more straightforward can be covered here. We start with the Positional Squeeze. Look at this ending:

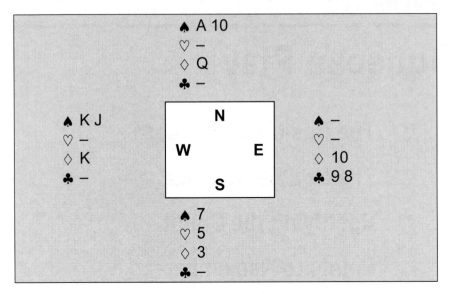

South cashes the five of hearts and what is West to do? If he throws the king of diamonds he establishes dummy's queen, so declarer throws the spade ten away and claims the last two tricks; if he pitches a spade, the diamond queen goes from the dummy and the ace and ten of spades make the last two tricks. This squeeze works because the defender had to play before declarer had to make the critical discard. Switch around the East and West hands and dummy must discard before the defender with the two stoppers, so the defender is under no pressure.

In the last example, North's spade ten and diamond queen were menaces (potential winners) against West, but would have been ineffective as menaces against East, had he held the defensive stoppers, or guards. The reason for the lack of effectiveness if the guards were sitting over the menaces was that both menaces were in the same hand. Now look at what happens if declarer has one menace in each hand.

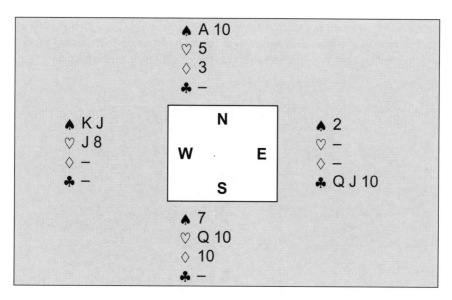

Declarer cashes the ten of diamonds and it does not matter which defender is guarding both majors; he will be squeezed into submission.

## The Double Squeeze

Then there is the Double Squeeze.

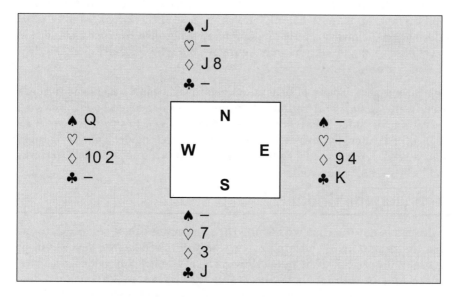

Declarer cashes the seven of hearts and first West is squeezed out of one of his diamonds so as to be able to keep the spade guard. The jack of spades has done its work now, so is pitched from the dummy, and the spotlight turns to East. He must keep the club king, so is also forced to discard a diamond. Declarer takes the last two tricks with the jack and eight of diamonds.

It is time to look at a complete deal.

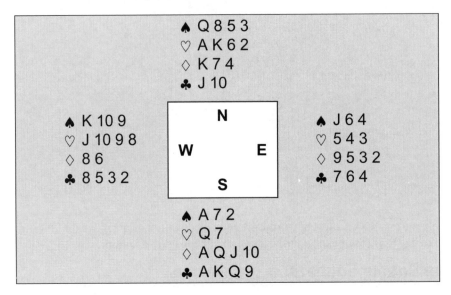

West leads the jack of hearts against the ambitious contract of Seven Diamonds. There appears to be only one chance; that the king of spades will fall under the ace. However, only one defender can guard the hearts, and if he also holds the spade king he may be in trouble when declarer cashes the minor-suit winners.

Declarer wins the queen of hearts to keep his communications as fluid as possible and cashes four rounds of trumps and the ace of spades followed by four rounds of clubs. The last club sees West obliged to throw a heart to keep the king of spades. Dummy's spade queen can no longer be of any value so away it goes, and the squeeze has seen to it that dummy's hearts are now all good to bring home the contract.

# Rectifying the Count

While this is not the case with some rare and more exotic squeezes, in most cases the squeeze will operate properly only where declarer has all but one of the remaining tricks. If he needs, say, nine of the last ten tricks, and has eight, a squeeze will rarely be successful. The reason is that each defender has an extra idle card, which will usually permit a painless discard. To tighten the screw, declarer has to give up a trick, such that he has eight winners but needs all of the last nine tricks. The technique involved in losing that necessary trick is known as Rectifying the Count. Look at this example:

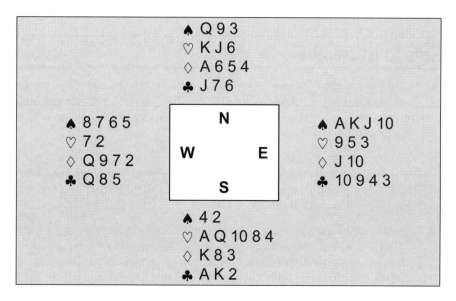

Playing in Four Hearts, declarer receives the lead of the seven of spades to East's ten. East continues with the ace and king of spades, declarer ruffing the third round high. Declarer draws trumps in three rounds and pauses to take stock. If the club queen falls in two rounds or the diamonds break three-three, there should be ten tricks. The only other hope is a squeeze if the same defender holds four diamonds and the queen of clubs.

To play ace, king and a third diamond would be a mistake. If the suit breaks four-two, the defender who wins the third round will play a fourth round, leaving no diamond menace for the endgame. As one trick must be lost even if the diamonds divide three-three, declarer plays a low diamond from each hand. Now he has all but one of the remaining tricks and needs them all. When East wins the diamond he returns a second diamond. Declarer wins the king to keep his communications open, then cashes the top clubs so that he will know what to discard on the last trump. Next comes that last trump. As West began with four diamonds and the queen of clubs, he is squeezed into submission. If he throws the club queen dummy pitches a diamond, while if he throws a diamond dummy throws the jack of clubs. Either way, declarer has his tenth trick.

# Points to Remember

♠ A squeeze occurs when one opponent has to guard two or more suits and cannot retain sufficient cards to do so. If declarer can cash sufficient winners in the other suits, sometimes the pressure proves to be too much for the defender to bear.

♠ For an effective squeeze, declarer must ensure that he has appropriate communications at the crucial point of the hand. Without them, the defender will be able to unguard the suit in which declarer cannot get at his potential extra winner.

♠ Some squeezes will work only against one specific opponent, while others will work against either. Careful planning and technique may make it possible to improve the chance of success by converting the first form into the latter. In particular, the Vienna coup may prove to be an effective tool with this in mind.

♠ Generally, declarer should need all but one of the remaining tricks for a squeeze to operate. Sometimes it will be necessary to go out of one's way to lose tricks early to rectify the count for the squeeze to work.

# Try it Yourself

In each case you are declarer, sitting South. How should you play to give yourself the best possible chance to make your contract?

## Question 1

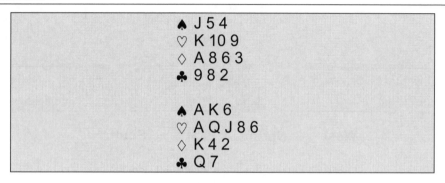

| West | North | East | South |
|------|-------|------|-------|
|      |       |      | 1♡    |
| Pass | 2♡    | 3♣   | 4♡    |
| All Pass |   |      |       |

West leads the six of clubs to the king. East cashes the club ace, West following with the four, then plays the club jack. Play on.

## Question 2

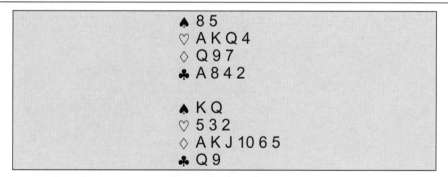

| West | North | East | South |
|------|-------|------|-------|
|      |       |      | 1◇    |
| Pass | 1♡    | Pass | 3◇    |
| Pass | 4◇    | Pass | 4♠ (i) |
| Pass | 6◇    | All Pass |   |

(i) Cuebid

West leads the jack of spades to the ace, East returning the two of spades.

## Question 3

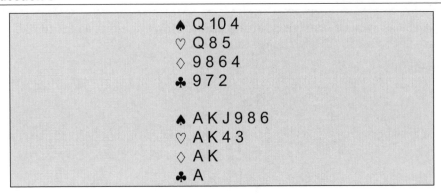

| West | North | East | South |
|------|-------|------|-------|
|      |       |      | 2♣ |
| Pass | 2♦ | Pass | 2♠ |
| Pass | 2NT | Pass | 3♡ |
| Pass | 4♠ | Pass | 4NT |
| Pass | 5♣ | Pass | 5NT |
| Pass | 7♠ | All Pass | |

West leads the king of clubs. When declarer starts on the trumps, West has all four of them.

## Question 4

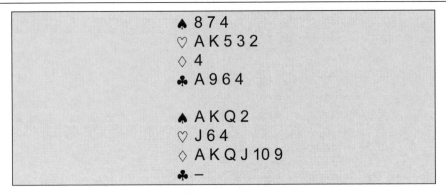

| West | North | East | South |
|------|-------|------|-------|
|      |       |      | 2♣ |
| Pass | 2♡ | Pass | 4♦ |
| Pass | 4♡ | Pass | 4NT |
| Pass | 5♡ | Pass | 7♦ |
| All Pass | | | |

The opening lead is the queen of clubs.

## Question 5

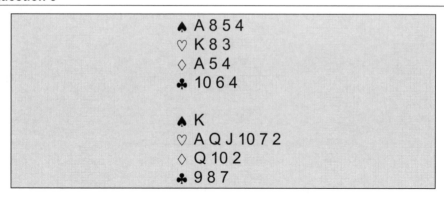

♠ A 8 5 4
♡ K 8 3
◊ A 5 4
♣ 10 6 4

♠ K
♡ A Q J 10 7 2
◊ Q 10 2
♣ 9 8 7

| West | North | East | South |
|------|-------|------|-------|
|      |       |      | 1♡    |
| 1♠   | 2NT   | Pass | 4♡    |
| All Pass |   |      |       |

West leads the king, queen and three of clubs to East's ace. East switches to a low trump. Play on.

## Question 6

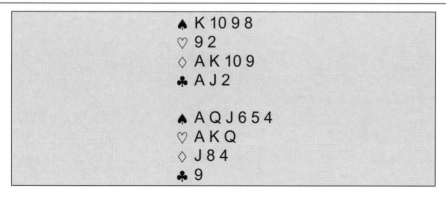

♠ K 10 9 8
♡ 9 2
◊ A K 10 9
♣ A J 2

♠ A Q J 6 5 4
♡ A K Q
◊ J 8 4
♣ 9

| West | North | East | South |
|------|-------|------|-------|
|      | 1NT(i) | Pass | 3♠   |
| Pass | 4♣    | Pass | 4♡    |
| Pass | 4NT   | Pass | 5♡    |
| Pass | 5NT   | Pass | 7♠    |
| All Pass |   |      |       |

(i) 15-17

The opening lead is the king of clubs.

## Question 7

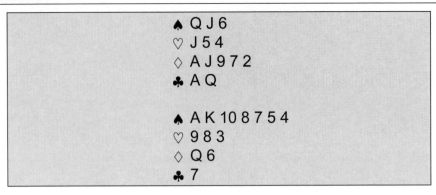

♠ Q J 6
♡ J 5 4
◇ A J 9 7 2
♣ A Q

♠ A K 10 8 7 5 4
♡ 9 8 3
◇ Q 6
♣ 7

| West | North | East | South |
|------|-------|------|-------|
|      |       | 1NT(i) | 2♠ |
| Pass | 4♠ | All Pass | |

(i) 15-17

West leads the ten of hearts. East wins the top three hearts and switches to a trump.

## Question 8

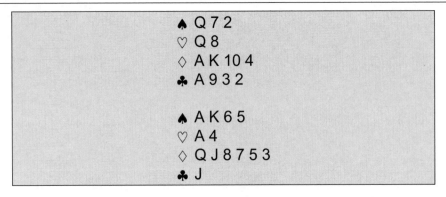

♠ Q 7 2
♡ Q 8
◇ A K 10 4
♣ A 9 3 2

♠ A K 6 5
♡ A 4
◇ Q J 8 7 5 3
♣ J

| West | North | East | South |
|------|-------|------|-------|
|      | 1NT(i) | Pass | 2♣ |
| Pass | 2◇ | Pass | 3◇ |
| Pass | 4◇ | Pass | 4NT |
| Pass | 5♡ | Pass | 5NT |
| Pass | 6◇ | Pass | 7◇ |
| All Pass | | | |

(i) 15-17

West leads the king of clubs.

## Question 9

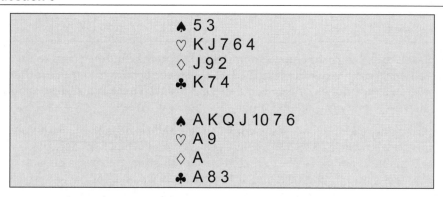

♠ 5 3
♡ K J 7 6 4
◇ J 9 2
♣ K 7 4

♠ A K Q J 10 7 6
♡ A 9
◇ A
♣ A 8 3

| West | North | East | South |
|------|-------|------|-------|
|      |       |      | 2♣    |
| Pass | 2♡    | Pass | 7♠    |
| All Pass |   |      |       |

The opening lead is the king of diamonds. If at some stage you play ace, king and ruff a heart, East shows up with queen, ten to four.

## Question 10

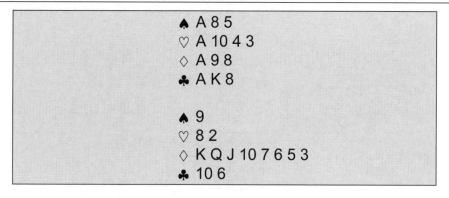

♠ A 8 5
♡ A 10 4 3
◇ A 9 8
♣ A K 8

♠ 9
♡ 8 2
◇ K Q J 10 7 6 5 3
♣ 10 6

| West | North | East | South |
|------|-------|------|-------|
|      | 1♣    | 2♡ (i) | 3◇  |
| Pass | 4NT   | Pass | 5♣    |
| Pass | 5NT   | Pass | 7◇    |
| All Pass |   |      |       |

(i) Weak

West leads the jack of hearts.

# Solutions

## Question 1

Declarer ruffs the third club high and draws trumps, finding them to be three-two, West having the length. The contract appears to require either a doubleton spade queen or an even diamond break. There is a third possibility, however, namely a spade-diamond squeeze on West.

Declarer ducks a diamond; East wins the ten and returns the jack of diamonds. Declarer wins the king, cashes the ace and king of spades, then cashes his last trump. If West started with both suits guarded, the last trump forces him to unguard one or the other. It was necessary to cash the ace and king of spades before playing the squeeze card, so that declarer would know what to discard from dummy on that trick. This play, creating a winner for the opponents, is known as a Vienna Coup. Had East returned a club instead of a diamond, West would have been squeezed on that trick, but declarer would have had to guess which suit he had unguarded.

## Question 2

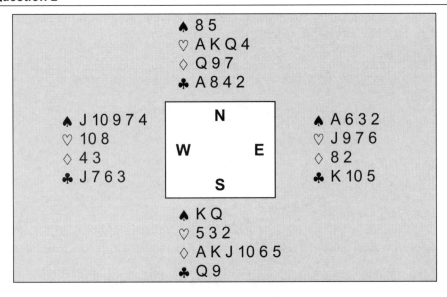

Declarer wins the spade return and takes two rounds of trumps, then cashes the ace of clubs before rattling off the rest of the trumps. If the hearts split three-three or the same defender holds both four hearts and the king of clubs, the contract will be made. Note again the Vienna Coup. If the ace of clubs is not cashed early, only a positional squeeze against West will operate, as the clubs will be blocked and East can afford to bare the club when the last trump is played. The Vienna Coup allows either defender to be squeezed.

## Question 3

There are twelve top tricks and a thirteenth may come from an even heart split or, perhaps, from drawing only two rounds of trumps then playing to ruff the fourth heart in the dummy. This does not look to be much of an extra chance, as giving West four-four in the majors leaves East with eleven cards in the minors, with which he might have interfered in the auction. A better extra chance is a red-suit squeeze against East.

Declarer cashes the ace and king of diamonds then crosses to dummy with a trump. Next he ruffs a diamond before running the trumps. If East did hold the length in both red suits he will be squeezed by the play of the last trump and either the diamond nine or fourth heart will prove to be a winner.

## Question 4

There will be thirteen tricks if either spades break three-three or the heart queen falls under the ace, king. What should declarer throw on the ace of clubs? Well, the odds are quite close between the two major suits, and to make a committal decision at trick one could be a fatal error.

Declarer should play low from dummy and ruff the club in hand. Then he cashes all the trumps, throwing two hearts, two clubs and a spade from dummy. Next he cashes the top hearts. If the queen falls, he throws the small spade on the ace of clubs. If the heart queen is still out, declarer throws the jack on the club ace and hopes to split the spades.

This line caters to both a three-three spade break and a doubleton heart queen, but it also succeeds when either defender began with four spades and the guarded queen of hearts, as he will have been squeezed. That is why it was essential to cash all the trumps before testing the hearts, as otherwise there would be no pressure on the defence.

## Question 5

On the assumption that West has at least five spades for his overcall, there will be a positional squeeze if he also holds the king of diamonds. Declarer wins the trump switch in hand and unblocks the king of spades. Now he plays two more rounds of trumps ending in dummy, and plays ace then ruffs a spade. The ruff isolates the menace. In other words, it ensures that only one defender is able to guard the suit, as it removes East's last spade. Now declarer runs the trumps. On the last one, West is squeezed. If he throws his last spade, dummy discards its remaining low diamond and the diamond ace and a spade win the last two tricks. If West hangs on to a spade, dummy's last spade is thrown away, having done its job. A low diamond lead sees the now bare king appear and dummy has a low diamond left to lead back to declarer's queen. As you will see, this time it was not possible to play the Vienna coup in diamonds, because the ace of diamonds was the only entry to the dummy.

## Question 6

It seems that the contract depends on the diamond finesse, but the opening lead improves declarer's chances somewhat on the reasonable assumption that West also holds the queen of clubs.

Declarer wins the ace of clubs, ruffs the low club, then runs all the trumps, followed by the three heart winners. The last winner squeezes West. Obliged to hang on to the queen of clubs, he has to come down to only a doubleton diamond. The club jack is now discarded and declarer plays on diamonds. There is no point in finessing when West cannot hold three cards, so he plays off the ace and king. The extra chance offered by this show-up squeeze is that declarer will drop a doubleton queen of diamonds offside. Of course, he was always going to succeed if the queen was with West.

## Question 7

West leads the ten of hearts. East wins the top three hearts and switches to a trump. East's opening bid marks the position of both the missing kings so there can be no successful finesse. A squeeze is possible, however. As East is sitting over dummy, one of declarer's menaces, or threat cards, must be in his own hand; otherwise East can just wait to see what dummy discards and follow suit to keep control.

A Vienna Coup will do the trick. Declarer wins the trump switch and cashes the ace of diamonds, leaving the queen as the threat card. Now he runs all the trumps, keeping ace, queen of clubs in the dummy. If the king of diamonds has not appeared, declarer leads to the ace of clubs at trick twelve, confident that the king will drop.

## Question 8

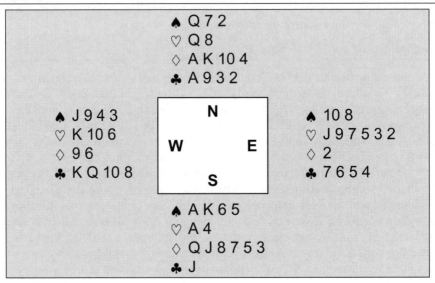

There are eleven winners, twelve via a spade ruff in the dummy, but prospects for a thirteenth by that route are not good, requiring a particularly unlikely distribution. Though this book is divided into ten sections, we have already discussed the fact that most hands require a combination of techniques, not only one. Here, the combination of dummy reversal and squeeze offers a much better chance of success.

Declarer wins the opening lead and ruffs a club, crosses to the diamond ten and ruffs a second club high. Another trump to dummy allows the last club to be ruffed. Declarer cashes the ace of hearts, Vienna Coup, and leads his last trump to dummy. Now dummy's fourth trump squeezes either defender if the heart king and four spades are together.

## Question 9

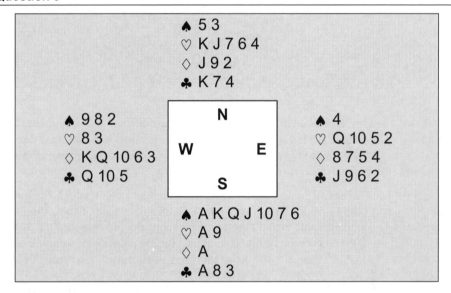

Declarer lacks the communications to establish and cash the fifth heart, but there is a very good chance for success nonetheless. Declarer wins the ace of diamonds and draws trumps before testing the hearts, ruffing the third round. The heart play has marked East with the defensive heart guard and the opening lead marks West with the diamond queen. The position looks to be ripe for a classic double squeeze.

Declarer cashes the rest of the trumps, coming down to king doubleton club and the two jacks in dummy. The last trump forces West to come down to a doubleton club to keep the diamond guard. Having done its work, the diamond jack is now discarded from the dummy. Now the attention turns to East. With the heart jack still sitting in dummy, he too is forced to come down to a doubleton club. Declarer plays club king and a club back to his ace, and the eight of clubs wins the last trick.

## Question 10

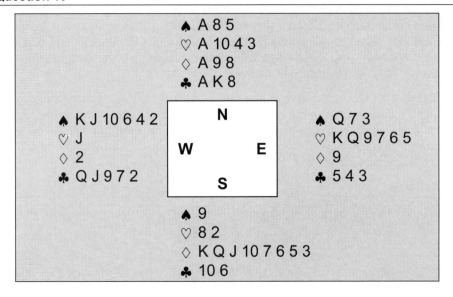

There are twelve top tricks and only a squeeze can deliver a thirteenth. East is known to have sole guard of the hearts. A squeeze will have to be a double squeeze, and will operate if West holds any six clubs or any number of clubs including the queen, jack and nine.

Declarer wins the ace of hearts and draws trumps in two rounds. Now he cashes the top clubs and leads dummy's last trump to get back to his hand. The rest of the trumps will crush the defenders should the missing cards be distributed as desired. When the last trump is led, West has two spades and a club honour. Forced to hang on to the club to guard against dummy's eight, he comes down to a singleton spade and dummy throws the now useless club away. East has come down to two spades also, along with a wining heart. Declarer's heart eight is a menace against East so he in turn must come down to only one spade. Declarer leads to the ace of spades and the dummy's remaining spade is good for the last trick.